PRACTICE GUIDE

VIOLIN

FOR USE WITH THE SUZUKI™
VIOLIN SCHOOL VOLUME 1

Shinichi Suzuki

"Anything you think of doing, however insignificant, should be done immediately. Spur yourself on and carry it through without becoming discouraged. If this becomes an ingrained habit, things you thought were impossible will become possible, and closed doors will open, as you will discover in many ways."

The music from Suzuki Violin School, Volume 1 is copyrighted by the International Suzuki Association and all rights are reserved. Any duplication of distribution of such material is expressly prohibited.

This work represents the view of its author and does not necessarily represent the view of the International Suzuki Association or its regional associations. These materials are not intended to replace authorized Suzuki® Method™ teacher training, study with a qualified Suzuki teacher, or Suzuki® Method™ core material, print or recorded.

Copyright © 2023 by Kari Spicer, Smart String Practice. All rights reserved.

No portion of this book may be reproduced in any form without written permission from the author, except as permitted by U.S. copyright law.

Contents

Welcome .... Page 1

The Violin .... Page 6

Practice & Games .... Page 12

Troubleshooting .... Page 27

Music .... Page 28

Playing .... Page 40

A Major .... Page 44

D Major .... Page 62

G Major .... Page 74

About Kari Spicer .... Page 90

Welcome Practice Partners!

Ready to become a better Practice Partner? This guide is designed to help you make practice better, and fun! I know it can be tough, and I also know that you CAN do this!

My goal with this guide is to help you be the best Practice Partner you can be, without overwhelming you. This guide can help you and your student to better understand everything new in the world of Violin and Suzuki.

My hope is that you will come back to this guide over and over as a quick reference to help you make the most of your student's lessons, and have fun and helpful practice sessions with your student.

HOW TO USE THIS GUIDE

1. **LEARN** - Look through the reference material and dig into any unfamiliar topics. Not understanding something? Ask your student's teacher!

2. **SCALES & ARPEGGIOS** - Become acquainted with Key Signatures, Scales, and Arpeggios. These are a great foundation for your student and becoming familiar with scales and arpeggios will help them play pieces better.

3. **GAMES** - Use practice games to make practice fun and helpful for your student. See the end of the book for game ideas!

4. **MAKE PRACTICE FUN** - Make practice more interesting by changing it up often for your student. Help them find games and activities that make practicing more enjoyable.

Enjoy this Adventure!

- Kari

What is a Practice Partner?

A Practice Partner is your student's "home coach."

A Practice Partner attends lessons with your student and practices with your student away from lessons.

Practice Partners are usually a parent or guardian, but could be any family member or friend with a commitment to attend lessons and regularly practice with your student.

A Practice Partner does not need any prior musical experience or need to know how to play the Violin.

A Practice Partner will:
- attend lessons and take notes (see Page 26)
- ensure practice happens
- prepare for practice (see Page 15)
- give guidance to what is practiced, based on lessons and notes
- make practice fun (see Games on Page 13)
- give encouragement and praise to the student

This Guide was developed specifically for Practice Partners, like you! Each section is designed to help you be a better Practice Partner, and thus help your student to improve and enjoy playing the Violin.

Instead of being written as a book to read cover to cover, feel free to jump around as needed to learn more of any areas of interest, especially where you may feel less familiar with a topic.

Suzuki Philosophy

Practice Partner Involvement - The Practice Partner attends all lessons, takes notes at lessons, and practices daily with the student.

Beginning Early - Although the early years are crucial for developing skills and coordination, it is never too late to start!

Listening - Listen daily to the recordings of the pieces being learned so you know what they sound like.

Repetition - The way we master a skill is by doing it over and over again. The student will continue to add pieces to their repertoire (vocabulary).

Encouragement - Celebrate your student's success and remember that each student learns at their own pace.

Learning with Other Children - Group Lessons and Performances are held where the student can learn by observing and interacting with other musicians.

Graded Repertoire - Each piece in the Suzuki repertoire is designed to teach a skill rather than just repeating boring exercises.

Delayed Reading - Just as a student learns how to speak their native tongue before they learn to read or write, your student will learn to read music in the same way with this complex instrument. Teachers may introduce music reading simultaneously, separately, or once the Violin feels more secure for the student.

Why Learn the Violin?

"Teaching music is not my main purpose. I want to make good citizens. If children hear fine music from the day of their birth and learn to play it, they develop sensitivity, discipline and endurance. They get a beautiful heart."

Shinichi Suzuki

Learning an instrument is more than just learning all the pieces and performing in front of an audience. What your student will gain from learning the Violin can enhance every aspect of their life.

Here are some traits and skills that are gained from learning the Violin:

- Hard work
- Following directions
- Learn about and explore creativity
- Find joy in music and an instrument
- Self-expression
- Systematic learning
- Perseverance
- Brain development
- Create art and beauty
- Cope with loss and heartache
- Use abilities for something greater
- Social Skills
- Develop coordination and posture

The Violin

Shinichi Suzuki

"A child's slowness in any subject indicates a deficiency in his environment, educational or otherwise."

Parts of the Violin

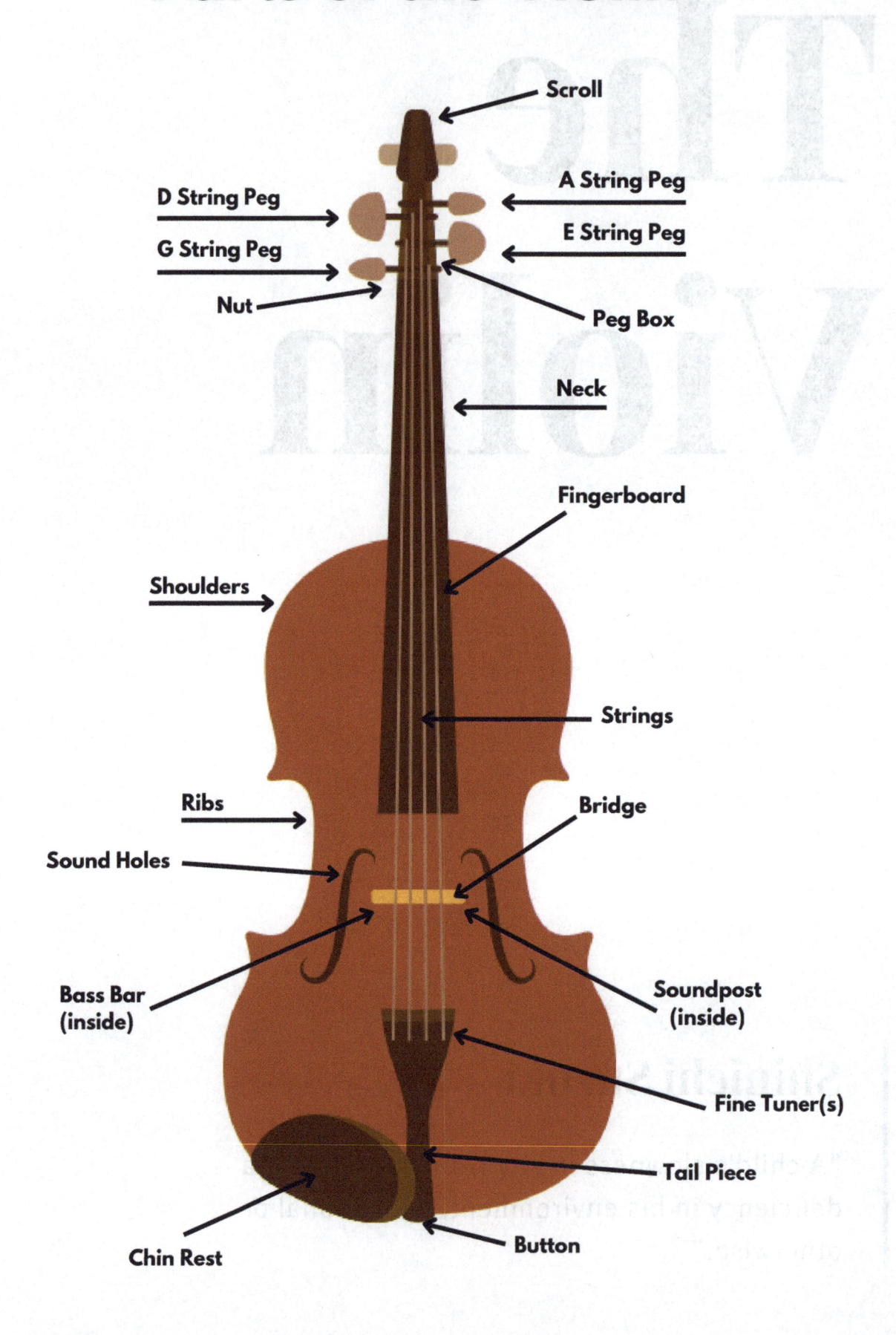

- Scroll
- D String Peg
- A String Peg
- G String Peg
- E String Peg
- Nut
- Peg Box
- Neck
- Fingerboard
- Shoulders
- Strings
- Ribs
- Bridge
- Sound Holes
- Bass Bar (inside)
- Soundpost (inside)
- Fine Tuner(s)
- Tail Piece
- Chin Rest
- Button

Parts of the Violin

Scroll - The head stock of the violin showcasing the Luthier's carving skills.

Peg Box and Pegs - The strings are wound on wooden pegs in the Peg Box. Raise or lower the string pitch by turning the peg.

Nut - Small piece of wood between the Peg Box and Fingerboard.

Neck - The area between the body and the Peg Box.

Fingerboard - Made of ebony, this is where the fingers are placed down on the strings.

Top and Back - Most violins are made of spruce wood on the top (where the sound holes are) and maple wood on the back.

Ribs - Thin strip of wood that binds the top and bottom of the violin together.

Strings (EADG) - Each string is a 5th apart. I recommend replacing strings once a year or more often as needed.

Sound Holes (f-holes) - The two holes on the top of the violin that look like a cursive "f" where the sound comes out.

Bridge - Transmits vibrations from the strings into the body of the instrument that create sound.

Bass Bar - Distributes the vibrations to the whole top of the instrument.

Soundpost - A wooden post made of spruce inside the violin. The way it connects to the top and back of the instrument can change the quality of the tone.

Fine Tuner(s) - Delicately adjust the pitch of the string. Smaller violins typically have a fine tuner on each string. A full size violin usually only has one fine tuner on the E string.

Tailpiece - Strings attach to this triangular piece of wood (plastic on smaller violins).

Chin rest - There are many different brands and styles of chin rests. The jaw fits on the chin rest more than the chin. A Shoulder Rest (not pictured) can also help for holding the violin correctly with good posture.

Button - Where the tailpiece connects to the violin.

Instrument sizes - 1/32, 1/16, 1/10, 1/8, 1/4, 1/2, 3/4, 4/4 (full size)

Parts of the Bow

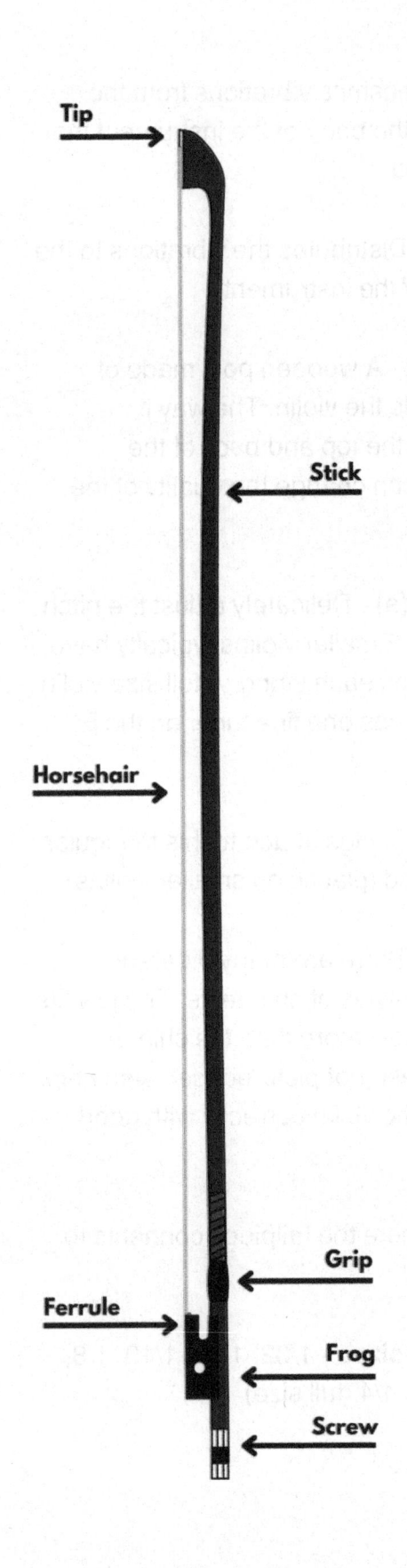

Tip →

Stick ←

Horsehair →

Ferrule →

← **Grip**

← **Frog**

← **Screw**

Stick - The quality of a bow is determined by the shape of the stick and the materials used.
- Wood - Preferred, has the best tone. Pernambuco (orange) and Brazilwood (brown).
- Carbon Fiber - Bounces nice, combo of carbon fiber and wood is best if you want a carbon fiber bow.
- Fiberglass - Cheapest, best for a child still learning to take care of equipment.

Do not use the bow to:
- Draw designs in the carpet
- Put the tip to the ground and lean on it like a cane
- Sword fights or Light Saber wars

Horsehair - The horsehair is what makes the beautiful sound. If oil from hands gets on the horse hair, it won't play.

Tip - The area where the stick and the horse hair come together. This is where bows tend to get weak and break.

Frog - A piece of wood attached to the bottom of the bow where the hair is attached.

Ferrule - A piece of metal that protects the place where the hair is attached to the bow.

Grip - The grip protects the stick.

Screw - Tightens and loosens the horsehair. A Bic pen is a good reference width for how tight the bow should be at the midpoint.

Bow re-hair - The hair on the bow does need to be replaced eventually, but for smaller bows, getting a new bow is typically less expensive.

Accessories

Chin rest and Shoulder rest - It is vital to get a chin rest and shoulder rest combo that fits best for proper technique and posture.

Foot chart - Your teacher may make you a foot chart with "Rest" and "Play" positions.

Case - The case will help protect the violin.

Rosin - Helps the hair to "stick" and pull the string. You want just enough rosin for the hair to grip the string and draw tone from the instrument. Too much rosin will create a static-like, fuzzy sound. You do not need to apply rosin every time, just when it feels like the bow is slipping from the strings. Check with your teacher for a high quality rosin that works best for your instrument.

Cleaning Cloth - After you are done practicing for the day, you will want to wipe down your instrument and bow. A microfiber cloth works best to clean the wood. If you have too much rosin residue it will affect the tone and can eventually stick to the varnish.

Recording Device - Record a video or take a picture of techniques your student's teacher is helping your student with so you can reference the technique during practice.

Notebook - Bring a notebook or a notes app to lessons so you can take notes about techniques, music, and what to practice. See page 26 for tips on taking notes during lessons.

Metronome - Tool to hear the tempo. Ask your teacher if you need a metronome.

Music Stand - You will want a higher quality music stand that is sturdy (not a wire stand). Ask your teacher when you should purchase a Music Stand.

Tuner - Tool to tune your instrument. Ask your teacher for a recommendation and how to tune with that tuner.

MakeMusic Cloud - Access practice tools and accompaniment recordings for Suzuki specific pieces. Visit MakeMusic.com/Suzuki to subscribe.

Care and Maintenance

Temperature and Humidity - Temperature and humidity changes will expand and contract wood. This can shift the soundpost inside of the Violin and the sound of your instrument may be affected. The pegs may also become loose, and the instrument will have a hard time staying in-tune.

Do not go from a humid climate to a dry climate without humidifying your Violin, as instruments like to be humid.

RECOMMENDATIONS: Never leave your Violin in the car overnight or for an extended period of time. Do not store your violin next to a vent, fireplace or windows.

Bows - Bows are much more fragile when they are tight and ready to play. If you have to leave your bow out, loosen it.

Deep Clean - Deep clean the wood of your Violin with varnish cleaner 3-4x per year. Clean strings with rubbing alcohol, but cover as much of the Violin so the alcohol doesn't get on the wood.

Bridge - The bridge is fragile. Care should be taken that it is not leaning too far beyond a slight angle away from the fingerboard. The feet of the bridge need to be completely flat. The strings tend to pull the bridge forward. If the bridge is leaning too much, the bridge can dent the Violin from where it was digging in and also warp the bridge.

Storage - I think most students would agree that the hardest part of practicing is getting the Violin out of the case and a close second is finding the most effective time of day to practice. This is why I recommend using a wall hook at home. It has been shown that students practice more when the instrument is in sight.

Ever since I was a little girl, my Violin has hung on a wall hook and now with my own children, I have hooks with their Violins on them and it makes it so much easier for me to get practice started.

RECOMMENDATIONS: It is tempting to put your Violin on the couch or a bed, but there are countless stories of instruments getting sat on. Make it a rule to never leave the Violin unattended except on the wall hook or in the storage case.

Practice & Games

Dieter Uchtdorf

"The desire to create is one of the deepest yearnings of the human soul."

Making Practice Fun!

"I love to practice!" This is what we want our students to say! Practice takes... practicing. Be patient with yourself. Review these principles often, and implement them consistently:

Make Practice a Joy
Practice should be about learning AND fun! Stay positive with your student and use a wide range of games and ways to practice, you can make each practice session a joy.

Your Teacher Knows Best
Remember that these are all ideas. You don't need to use any of them, or you could use all of them, or any variety in between. These are not meant to to override your teacher's guidance, they are to support their teaching. Your teacher knows your student best!

Consistency
Your student will thrive when there is consistency in daily practice. This daily routine becomes a foundation your student can count on each day, and even look forward to.

Practice, not Perfection
Keep your expectations reasonable. Your student doesn't need to be perfect, they just need to practice and find joy in it.

Accomplishments, not Time
Instead of focusing on a set amount of time, make practice sessions revolve around a reasonable accomplishment. Your student's teacher can help you choose accomplishments to focus on in practice sessions.

Keep It Short
Practicing is more fun when it is short in duration, even if that means practicing several times a day for a few minutes. As your student gets older, practice time should get longer.

Be Positive and Compliment
Encourage your student and compliment them often, even on the little things. Small successes will help your student to enjoy practice and learning the Violin.

Games
Always have games on hand! Have enough games to switch them up, give your student a choice of what game to play, and to keep practice sessions fun and interesting.

What is Practice?

Practicing is more than just playing through a piece. Practice is about isolating the root of the problem. Practice involves playing a segment repeatedly until it becomes easier and automatic.

How do I know what to practice?
Your teacher will give you behaviors, segments, and skills to work on in lessons. These are what to focus on during practice until it becomes easier.

Repetition is Key
Repetition is key to proper practice. With repetition, skills become easy and automatic and ready to build upon. Repetition is also important for building your student's repertoire by reviewing the pieces your student already knows.

Pause and Reflect
Every part of practice should include the principle of pausing and reflecting. Taking a moment to pause and reflect allows the student and practice partner to process what was just done and evaluate what step comes next.

Practice in Chunks
Practice in small chunks, focused on a skill or segment of a piece, with clear directions. Playing a whole piece does not make for a useful practice session.

Daily Practice
Keeping a pattern of daily practice will help your student retain what is learned. Irregular practice and skipped days of practice will set your student back.

Practicing after your Lesson
The best practice you and your student will have is right after a lesson with your student's teacher. This is when things will be the most fresh and easiest to remember.

How Many Repetitions?
The smaller the behavior, segment, or skill, the more repetitions. If the task is larger, do less repetitions.

Difficulty Following Directions
If your student has difficulty following directions, this is a clear sign that this is more than they can do at this time. Find a way to simplify the task to even more simple or smaller parts.

Practice Preparation

Practice Room
Find a small, focused space as a "Practice Room" for your student. Choose a space that is quiet, with minimal distractions, and keep the space clean and organized. Most practices should occur in this space, but it can be fun to mix it up and use another space at times.

Supplies Ready
Have a bag or storage container ready to go with all the supplies you need for a practice session so everything is ready to go.

Keep Sessions Short
Short practice sessions will help keep your student's focus and attention. Practicing several times a day for a short amount of time is far better than one long practice session.

Consistent Time, Yet Flexible
Having a consistent time for practice will help make practice easier for your student to do every day, and minimize the complaints about having to practice. Be flexible as needed, making practice essential but the time is flexible for important events.

Goal in Mind
Before each practice session, have a goal in mind of what you want your student to accomplish. Make the goal reasonable, and be positive even if your student does not accomplish the goal during practice.

Observing
Pay close attention during lessons how your teacher works with your student, especially when showing details such as fingers, hands, movements, etc. Ask your teacher if you can observe another student or watch practice videos on YouTube. The more you can observe, the better your practice sessions can be.

Focus
Your student can best focus when they are given an inviting environment and a willing practice partner. This allows your student to find the inner calmness necessary to learn.

Trust the Process
You are only responsible for your behavior during practice. Your student's behavior can be influenced by you, but it is not your responsibility. Be patient, be kind, trust the process.

Practice Rewards

Creating a practice reward system for your student will motivate them to practice and become more proficient. This reward system is separate from any reward system your student's teacher may use.

One example of a practice reward system can be a "Store." Students earn tickets during practice, immediately after a task is performed correctly. Students can redeem a certain number of tickets for items from the store once a week on an established day (i.e. Fridays). The store may have physical items, digital items, or experiences at differing amounts of tickets. This reward system gives both instant feedback and delayed gratification.

There may be many different types of practice reward systems, but these are the principles any system should follow:

Age appropriate - The younger the student, the more fast-paced reward system they need.

Visual or Tangible - Giving students a reward they can see or hold makes the reward feel real.

Track one behavior at a time - both of you have a clear understanding of what one behavior needs to happen for a single task (i.e. stop at the end of a segment). Do not worry about any other behaviors or skills besides the one behavior.

Reward immediately - gives a student instant feedback

Positive reinforcement - let your student know what they did correctly more than what they are doing wrong

Keep it simple - lectures don't change behavior

Avoid bribery - stay away from offering a reward in the middle of incorrect behaviors or skills. Rewards should be planned before a task is started.

Number Line Games

Repetition is a BIG part of learning the Violin. Instead of focusing on really hard things, focusing on repetition creates a strong foundation for your student to help them progress and advance with their instrument.

You can find ready-to-go repetition games at SmartStringPractice.com where all you have to do is print and cut! You can also scan the QR code with your phone on each games page to see all the options for the game type.

Number Line games are great for teaching students to do their very best for every repetition, because if they don't they will be set back and need to make up the repetition to keep progressing. Spice up practices with fun and variety with number line games on my website!

How to Play:
Set out the numbers from 10 down to -3 and have your student start at 0.

Pick a skill or small segment of a piece.

For each correct repetition, the student moves up a number. For each incorrect repetition, the student moves down a number.

The goal is for the student to get to number 10.

Hot Dog Boogie - A Number Line Game

Bucket Games

Bucket Games can be played with small items like pennies or for variety and fun, find printable Bucket Games on my website.

How to Play:
Pick a skill or small segment of a piece.

Start with a pile of items, with fewer items for larger skills and more items for smaller skills.

For every correct repetition, place an item in the student's pile. If the repetition is done incorrectly, place an item in the practice partner's pile.

An item in the practice partner's pile can be moved to the student's pile after a correct repetition.

The goal is for the student to get all the items in their own pile.

Basketball Madness - A Bucket Game

Counting Games

Counting Games can make repetitions fun by marking off a chart or gathering items as a skill or piece segment is played correctly.

How to Play:
Pick a skill or small segment of a piece.

Select a chart or item to count. See SmartStringPractice.com for a variety of printables to help make this easy and fun. Start with fewer items for larger skills and more items for smaller skills.

For each correct repetition of the skill or segment piece, have your student mark the chart or move an item.

The goal is for the student to mark off the full chart or move all the items.

Feed the Dinosaurs!

Feed the Dinosaurs!
100x

Gumballs Galore

Spelling Games

Spelling Games are a fun way to fit in repetitions for skills or segments of pieces. Ready-to-go Spelling Games can be found at SmartStringPractice.com.

How to Play:
Pick a skill or small segment of a piece.

Pick letters to spell your student's name or a familiar word. If your student does not know how to spell yet, they can still play this game and just match the shapes of letters. My website SmartStringPractice.com has many options for ready-to-go and fun Spelling Games.

Start the student with the faded version of the letters. You can have it spelled out correctly, or for a challenge mix up the letters and have them guess the word.

For every correct repetition, give the student a full version of the letter and have them set it on top of the faded version. For an incorrect repetition, take back the full version.

The goal of Spelling Games is for the student to get in repetitions by collecting all the full version letters and to spell the word.

Day at the Beach - A Spelling Game

Puzzle Games

Puzzle Games are a fun way to fit in repetitions.

How to Play:
Pick a skill or small segment of a piece.

Make a puzzle similar to the one below or download one of our fun puzzles at SmartStringPractice.com.

Have your student do the skill or play the segment. For every correct repetition, the student gets a piece of the puzzle. For every incorrect repetition, take a puzzle piece away.

For very young students, consider giving out the puzzle in order. For all other students, give them the puzzle pieces in random order for them to piece together.

The goal of Puzzle Games is to get reptitions in and to assemble the full puzzle.

Winter Puzzle - A Puzzle Game

Progression Games

How to Play Progression Games:
Select a practice spot and download a Progression Game from SmartStringPractice.com.

Divide the section or piece into several segments.

Your student should have some proficiency with each segment before playing a progression game, because this game is focused on combining segments together.

- Ensure your student can play the 1st and 2nd sections independently.
- Now we want to play the segments together!
- Play the 1st section, pause, play the 2nd section, and pause. Repeat until several correct repetitions are achieved.
- Now play the 3rd section independently. Repeat until several correct repetitions are achieved.
- Then play the 1st section, pause, play the 2nd section, pause, play the 3rd section, and pause. Repeat until several correct repetitions are achieved.
- Repeat this pattern until all sections have been played.
- Lastly, play all sections together without pausing in between.

The goal is to become more familiar with the segments of a piece, to play each segment clean, and to smoothly transition from each segment to the next.

Flower Garden - A Progression Game

Recipe Games

Recipe Games are a fun way for your student to get in more repetitions for a skill or playing a segment of a piece.

How to Play:
Pick a skill or small segment of a piece.

Find ingredients to create a recipe or download a ready-to-go Recipe Game from SmartStringPractice.com.

Have your student do the skill or play the segment. For every correct repetition, the student gets to add an ingredient (or section of the pizza in the example below). For every incorrect repetition, take a piece away.

The goal of Recipe Games is to get in more repetitions in a fun way by adding all the ingredients in the recipe!

Pizza Builder - A Recipe Game

More Game Ideas

Stuffed Animal Concert
Gather a bunch of stuff animals and line them up as an audience. Then choose an activity or repetition game and perform for the audience. Bravo!

Lego Creations
Pick something to build (i.e. house, car, helicopter) and use Legos or building blocks to create it. Each correct repetition gives your student one more piece to assemble the item.

Dress a Doll or Stuffed Animal
With a doll or stuffed animal and some dress up clothes, have your student add one item of clothing for every correct repetition. For an incorrect repetition, you could have them remove an item.

Tall Tower
With blocks or items that can be stacked safely, have your student add one item for each correct repetition, and remove an item for each incorrect repetition. Make a goal to build the tower to a certain height (your child's height, the height of a table, etc.).

Flashlight Game
With a flashlight, flash once for a correct repetition and twice for an incorrect repetition. Set a time or count to a goal number to know when to complete this game.

Just a Minute!
With a timer, see how many times In 1 minute your student can play a piece segment or perform a skill correctly. For added fun, keep track of these numbers to see progress!

Hot and Cold
Have your student hide a metronome or pencil somewhere in the room while you are not looking. Look for the hidden item. As you get closer, your student can play a segment louder. As you get further from the item, your student can play the segment softer.

Reviewing & Listening

Reviewing and listening are pillars of practice, and are designed to make learning the Violin easier and faster.

Reviewing

Review is a very important aspect of Suzuki. Review is the repetition of older pieces. Review develops skills through repetition and makes learning new skills easier.

Review is often ignored or done incorrectly, as many students either focus on new pieces or play casually through old pieces.

Reviewing pieces can give confidence to your student. A natural outcome of your student playing a piece they are familiar with is the feeling that they are good at this! This gives them a chance to show off, even without an audience.

Answers to challenging segments of new pieces can often be answered through reviewing older pieces. Your student's repertoire becomes a wealth of experience for learning new pieces.

Your student will also benefit from reviewing by seeing how far they have progressed and it will help them to love playing even more.

Listening

Think of music your student may listen to on the radio for fun. The songs they enjoy the most are the songs they are most familiar with, and listen to over and over. This same principle applies in learning the Violin.

Listening can be done as a focused task, as well as just background music in the car or at home.

It is much easier to get to a destination when you know where you are going. Listening allows your student to know the destination, even when they are not able to play it proficiently. The purpose of practice is to get your student to arrive at that destination!

Taking Notes at Lessons

Look for a Theme
With young children especially, look for a theme or something repeated by the teacher and circle that in your notes.

Step by Step
Be specific when a teacher breaks up a technique into steps or segments. Write down each step so you can help your student repeat this in practice.

Take Note of Cues
Stay focused during lessons and look for "cues" that your student's teacher may give. Listen for the word "practice" and descriptive or comparison language. Take note of "locations" in the music, such as a specific measure.

Ask Questions
If you are unsure about a task or segment, ask your student's teacher for clarification, or about how you can best practice this at home with your student.

Record Audio or Video
Use a phone or camera to capture positions, segments, or behaviors for reviewing during practice. This will help you better understand how to best recreate what your teacher worked on during lessons.

Lesson Check-ins
Discuss with your student's teacher the best time to check-in with questions about practice at home and assignments. This could be at the beginning or end of a lesson, or another scheduled time.

Troubleshooting

If your student says: "I don't want to practice today," or "I hate playing this instrument," or "This is too hard," or something similar, here are some ideas to better understand the root cause of the issue.

Listen and Understand
The first words they are saying are likely not the issue. Take a break, go out somewhere different, and take a little time to discover the root of the problem by listening.

Don't try to fix it, just listen and understand. After they share, ask if they can think of a solution to the problem and discuss it. If needed, ask if you can share an idea for a solution.

Physical Issues to Consider
Could your student be hungry, tired, upset about something from school or a friend, or some other physical issue? Does your student have a pressing project that is stressing them out? Be proactive and help your student to have a snack, get enough rest, etc. so they can better focus on meaningful activities, including lessons and practice.

"I don't want to play the Violin anymore"
Your student may be altogether so frustrated they want to stop playing or change instruments. Understanding what is causing them to feel this way can lead you to helping them find a workable solution to the core issue.

"I don't like my teacher"
Students may get frustrated with their teacher or become negative towards their teacher for some reason. Changing teachers will usually not fix the core issue. The first step is to understand the core issue your student is facing. Work together to find a reasonable solution. As needed, discuss the situation with their teacher privately and work as a team to find a reasonable solution.

"Playing the Violin is too hard"
Actually, it's true! The Violin is one of the hardest instruments to master, but so good for the mind. Learning the Violin takes a lot of hard work, time, focus, and dedication. Learning how to work hard is one of the best ways students can grow and become independent in all areas of life and give them confidence.

Music

Shinichi Suzuki

"Where love is deep, much can be accomplished."

Sound and Tone

Tone - The quality of the sound

Intonation
- Higher = if the pitch needs to go higher, the finger moves closer to the bridge
- Lower = if the pitch needs to go lower, the finger moves closer to the scroll

Bow Hold
- Outside: thumb is on the ferrule
- Inside: thumb is on the grip/stick

Choosing your instrument
- You should get the highest quality instrument you can afford. It will have a better tone and you'll be more motivated to listen in the early days of practicing and train your ear to hear the best quality.

Down Bow
Opening up the elbow, frog going towards the ground. The symbol that tells us to use a down bow in music looks like this:

Up Bow
Elbow closing, tip going higher in the air. The symbol that tells us to use an up bow in music looks like this:

Reading Notes and Rests

Note		Rest	Duration
Whole Note	𝅝	𝄻	4 beats
Half Note	𝅗𝅥	𝄼	2 beats
Dotted Quarter Note	♩.	𝄽.	1 ½ beats
Quarter Note	♩	𝄽	1 beat
8th Note	♪ or ♫	𝄾	½ beat
8th Note Triplet	♫♪ (3)	𝄽	1 beat
16th Note	♬ or ♬♬	𝄿	¼ beat

Time Signatures

Signature	Description
C	**Common Time** The most "common" time, also known as 4/4 time. Four quarter notes per measure.
4/4	**4/4 Time** Also known as "common time." Four quarter notes per measure.
¢	**Cut Time** Similar to Common Time but "slashed" in half, so it goes twice as fast. Two half notes per measure.
3/4	**3/4 Time** Three quarter notes per measure.
2/4	**2/4 Time** Two quarter notes per measure.

Musical Terms

DYNAMICS — When the music gets louder or softer

p — **Piano**, meaning "quiet"

mp — **Mezzo piano**, meaning "moderately quiet"

mf — **Mezzo forte**, meaning "moderately loud"

f — **Forte**, meaning "loud or strong"

TEMPO

A tempo	**In time,** meaning return to original speed
Allegro	**Fast, quickly, bright,** around 120-156 bpm
Allegretto	**Moderately fast, but less than allegro,** around 100-128bpm
Allegro moderato	**Moderately fast,** around 130-150 bpm
Andante	**A walking pace,** around 72-76 bpm
Andantino	**Slightly faster, more light-hearted than Andante,** about 73-83 bpm
Cantabile	**Singable or Songlike**
Martelé	**Hammered,** a percussive bow stroke
Meno mosso	**Slower**
metronome	**Tool to hear the tempo in beats per minute (bpm)**
Moderato	**At a medium tempo**
Sempre Staccato	**Play staccato for the entire section**

Musical Terms

OTHER

arco	**Played with the bow**
detaché	**Broad, but separate bow strokes**
dim	**Gradual decrease in volume**
dolce	**Smooth, soft**
Fine	**The end**
D.C. al Fine	**Play from beginning to end, skip any repeats**
pizzicato (pizz. or +)	**Use finger to pluck the string**
poco rit	**A little slow-down**
ritardando (rit)	**Gradually decreasing in tempo**
sempre	**Consistently**

Musical Symbols

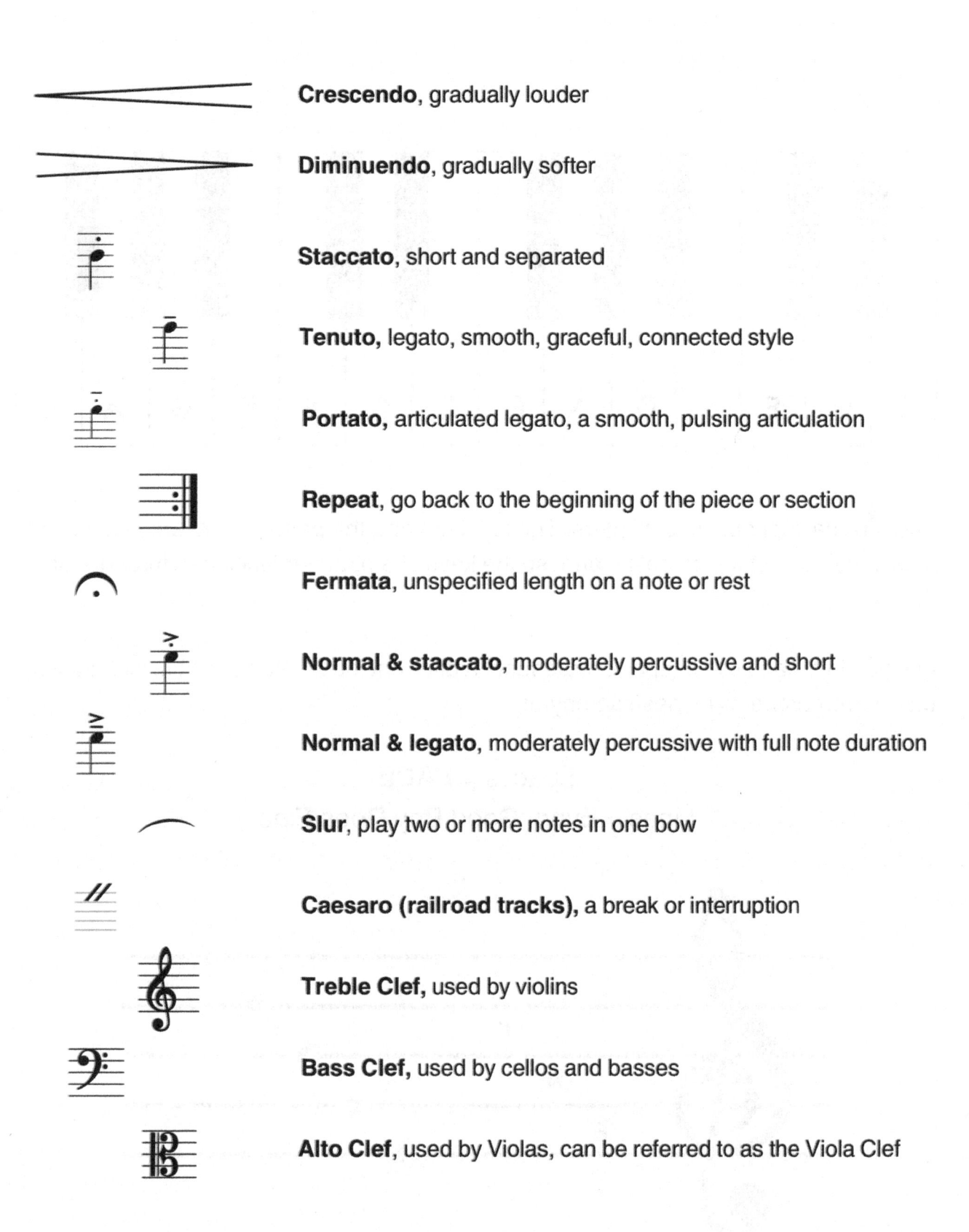

Crescendo, gradually louder

Diminuendo, gradually softer

Staccato, short and separated

Tenuto, legato, smooth, graceful, connected style

Portato, articulated legato, a smooth, pulsing articulation

Repeat, go back to the beginning of the piece or section

Fermata, unspecified length on a note or rest

Normal & staccato, moderately percussive and short

Normal & legato, moderately percussive with full note duration

Slur, play two or more notes in one bow

Caesaro (railroad tracks), a break or interruption

Treble Clef, used by violins

Bass Clef, used by cellos and basses

Alto Clef, used by Violas, can be referred to as the Viola Clef

Musical Alphabet

A B C D E F G

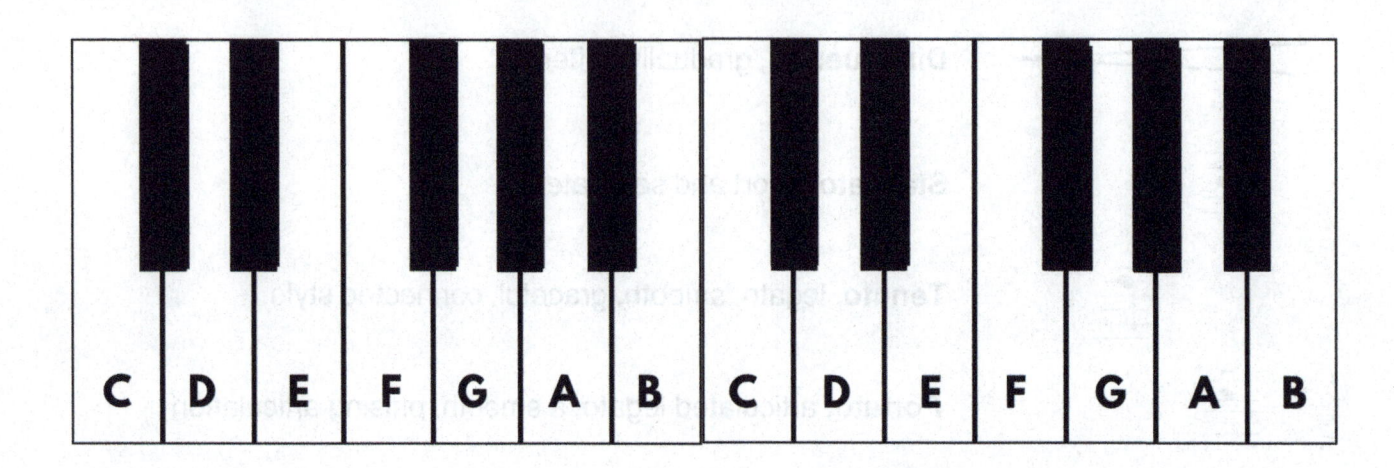

C D E F G A B C D E F G A B

The musical alphabet has 7 letters. These letters and the patterns that are laid out in music are easiest to see on a piano, so the keys of a piano are included throughout this book.

On the staff, each line or space represents a different letter. For the treble clef, this is easy to remember with these acronyms:

Spaces = **FACE**
Lines = **E**very **G**ood **B**oy **D**oes **F**ine

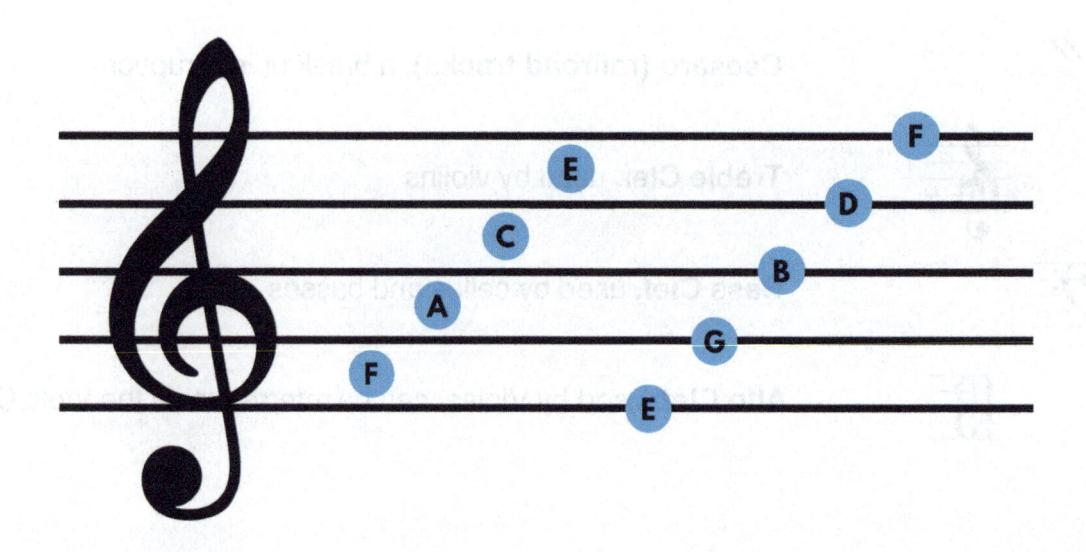

Key Signatures

A Key Signature is a set of seven notes from the musical alphabet. Notes may be natural, flat, or sharp. The flats and sharps in the key signature are indicated next to the treble clef.

Each key signature has a different feel. Major key signatures have a "happy" feel, and Minor key signatures have a more "sad" feel.

This book will focus on **A Major**, **D Major**, and **G Major**.

Each Major key signature and accompanying pieces will use the same color throughout this book.

A Major   A B C# D E F# G# A

D Major   D E F# G A B C# D

G Major   G A B C D E F# G

Musical Notes

The placement of the sharp or flat on the staff is telling you which note is sharp or flat.

Natural

A note with no symbol or a "natural" symbol is found on the "white" keys of the piano. These notes are called by just the letter, such as "A" or "B."

The "natural" symbol is used when a note has a sharp or flat from the Key Signature but is intended to not be played as sharp or flat.

Sharp

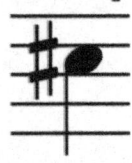

A note with a "sharp" symbol is a half step above a natural note, and is found on the "black" keys of the piano.

Flat

A note with a "flat" symbol is a half step below a natural note, and is found on the "black" keys of the piano.

Scales

Music is made up of scales and arpeggios.

Scales are made up of WHOLE (⊔) and HALF (∨) steps.
W   H

If the pattern of whole and half steps sounds "happy" it is in a MAJOR KEY.

Scales tell us all the notes we will play in a specific key signature.

Every scale has a finger pattern the student will use to play each piece.

In Suzuki Violin Book 1, the student will learn pieces first in **A Major**, then **D Major**, and finally **G Major**.

Whole and half steps are easiest to see on the piano. In the Key of **A Major**, It looks like this:

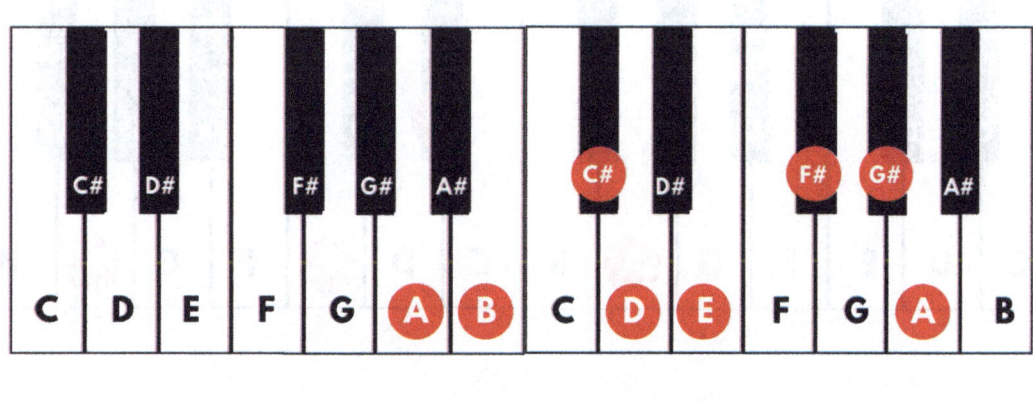

A B C# D E F# G# A
W W H W W W H

Arpeggios

When certain notes of a scale are played at the same time, it is called a chord.

A string instrument plays the notes of a chord one after the other instead of all at the same time. **This is called an arpeggio.**

Many arpeggios are found within each piece.

Knowing the arpeggios can help a student focus on other techniques that add to the details of each piece.

An arpeggio in **A Major** on the piano, looks like this:

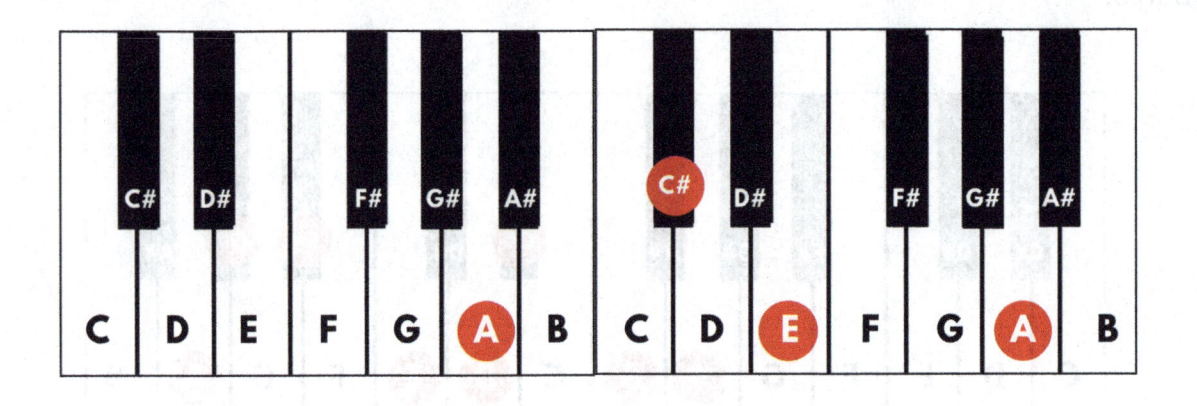

39

Playing

Robert Duke

"Skill acquisition is a process of developing habit's strength through consistent repetition over time."

Violin Fingerboard

As you will notice, there are not any markings on the neck of the Violin. This makes it difficult to know finger placement.

Your teacher may put a first finger, second finger, and third finger tape on your Violin. If needed, a 4th finger tape may be added as well. A fingerboard is an easy way to see tapes, finger placements, and notes:

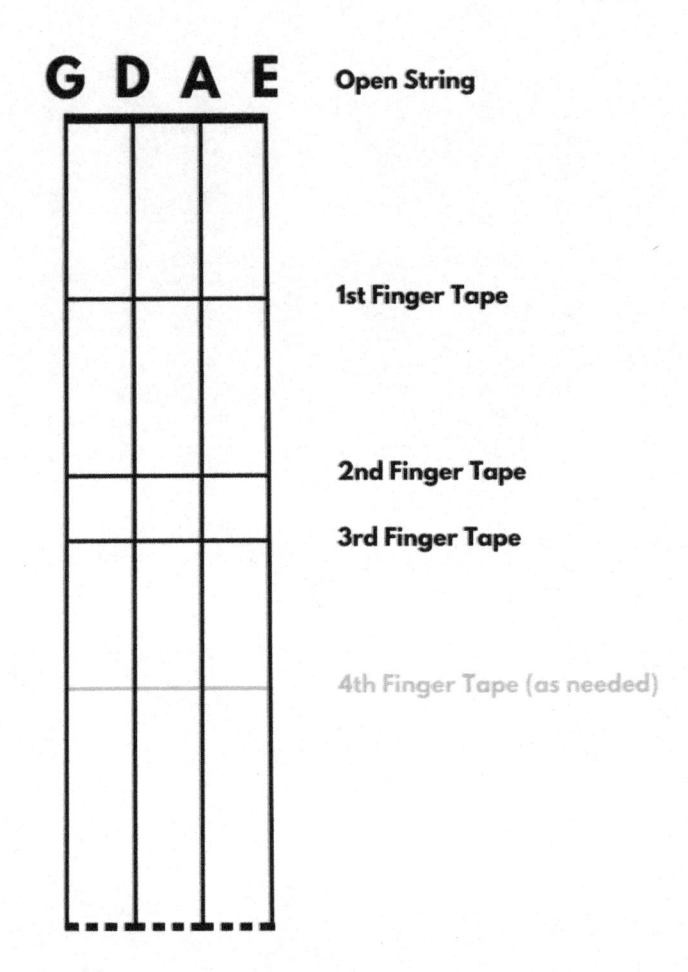

G D A E Open String

1st Finger Tape

2nd Finger Tape

3rd Finger Tape

4th Finger Tape (as needed)

The space between the Open String and the 1st Finger Tape is a whole step.
The space between the 1st Finger Tape and the 2nd Finger Tape is a whole step.
The space between the 2nd and 3rd Finger Tapes is a half step.
The space between the 3rd and 4th Finger Tapes is a whole step.

The 4th finger is the same note as the open string with the matching letter name. Your teacher may want you to use a 4th finger instead of an open string, ask for clarification!

Violin Finger Placement

A fingerboard will show you the notes played at a specific string and finger placement.

The horizontal lines on a fingerboard represent finger tapes.

The letters at the top are the notes for the open string (no fingers on the string).

The circles represent the notes played at a specific string and finger placement.

Only the notes and open strings that are played will be colored and shown.

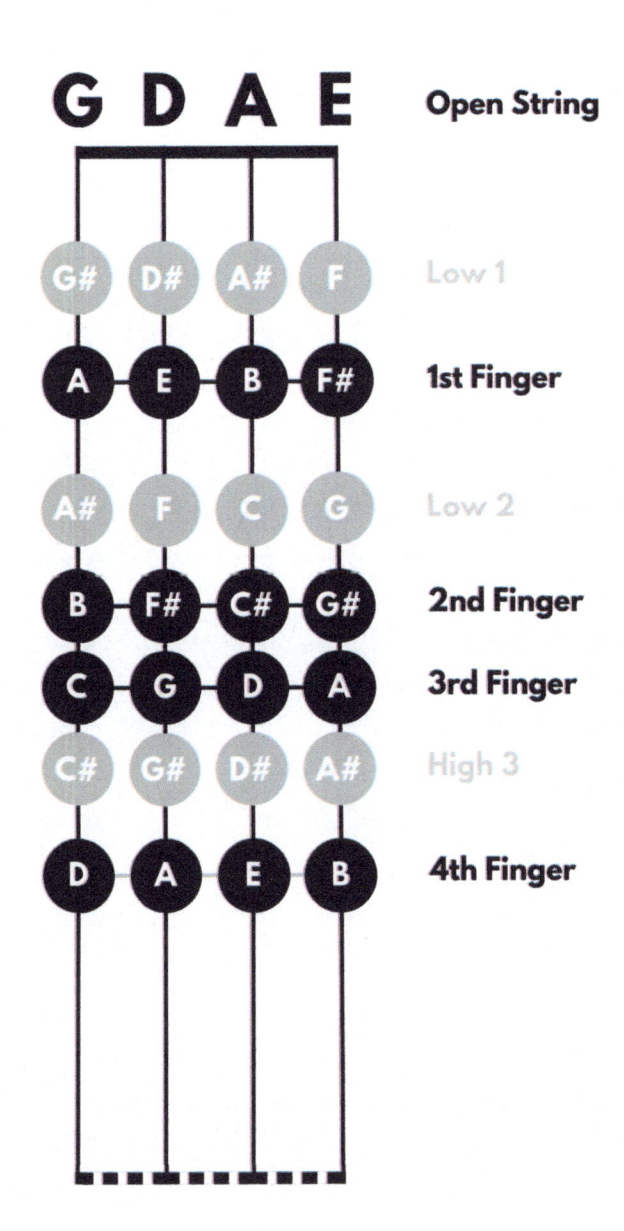

G	D	A	E	Open String
G#	D#	A#	F	Low 1
A	E	B	F#	1st Finger
A#	F	C	G	Low 2
B	F#	C#	G#	2nd Finger
C	G	D	A	3rd Finger
C#	G#	D#	A#	High 3
D	A	E	B	4th Finger

A Major

A Major

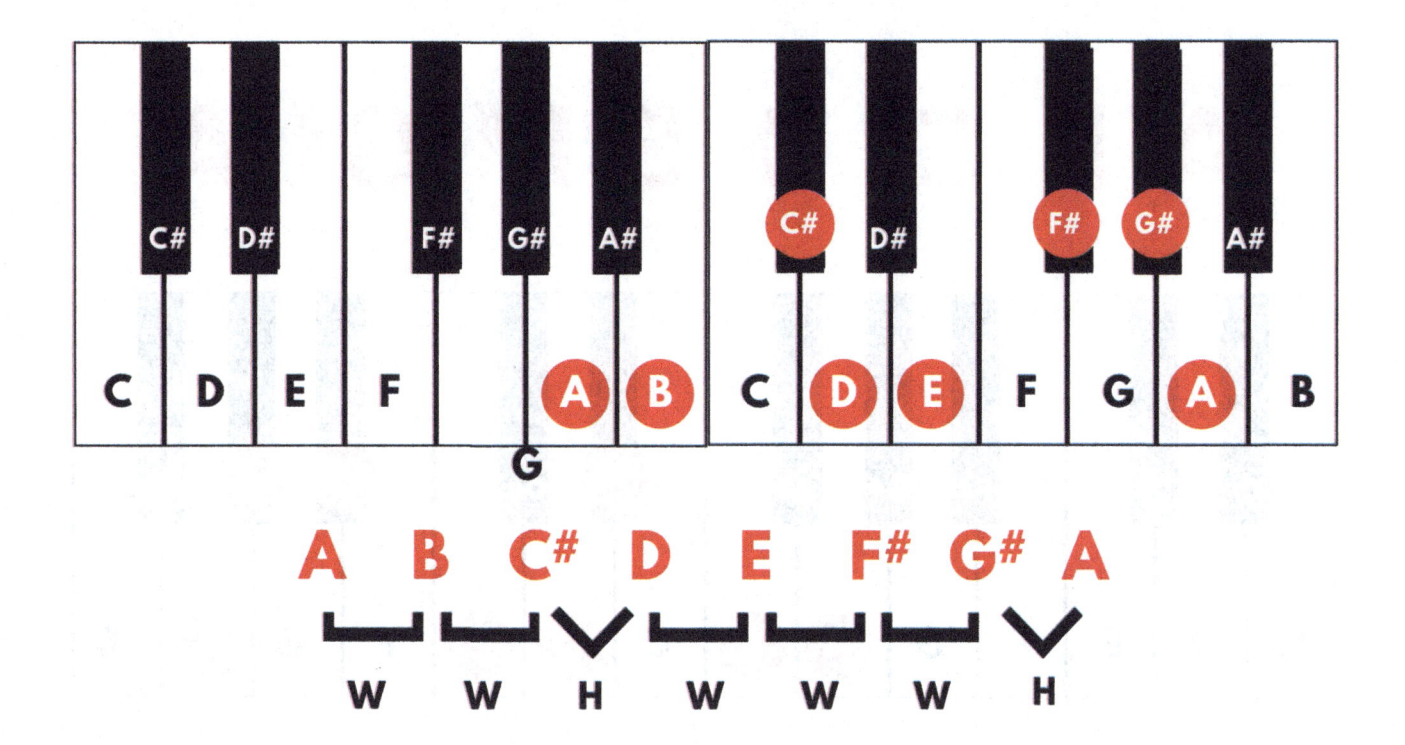

A B C# D E F# G# A

W W H W W W H

Pieces in Book 1 in A Major:

1. Twinkle, Twinkle, Little Star Variations
2. Lightly Row
3. Song of the Wind
4. Go Tell Aunt Rhody
5. O Come, Little Children
6. May Song
7. Long, Long Ago
8. Allegro
9. Perpetual Motion

A Major Scale

A B C# D E F# G# A

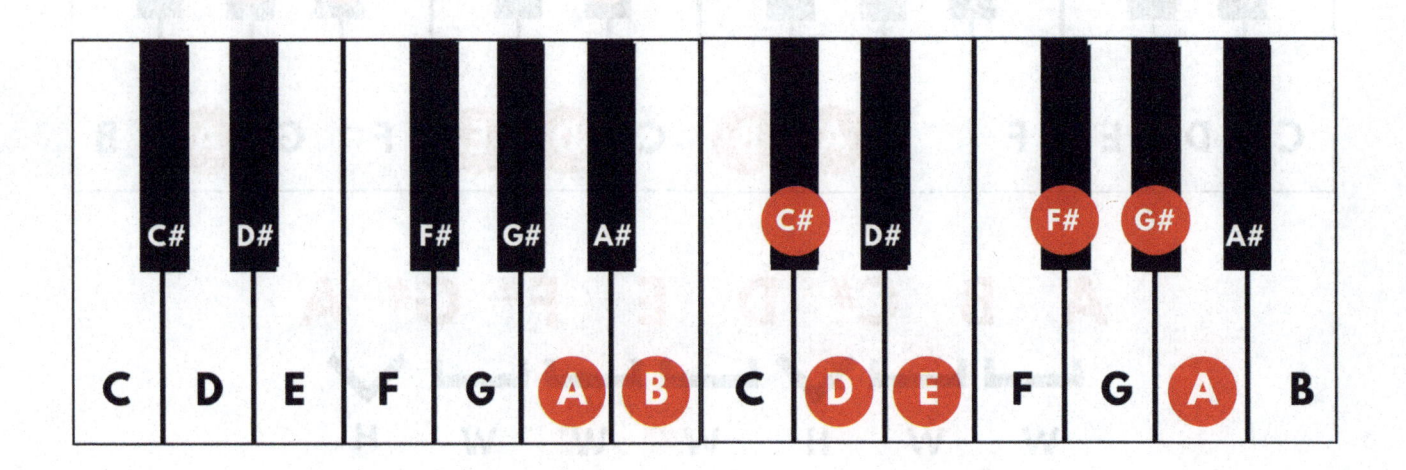

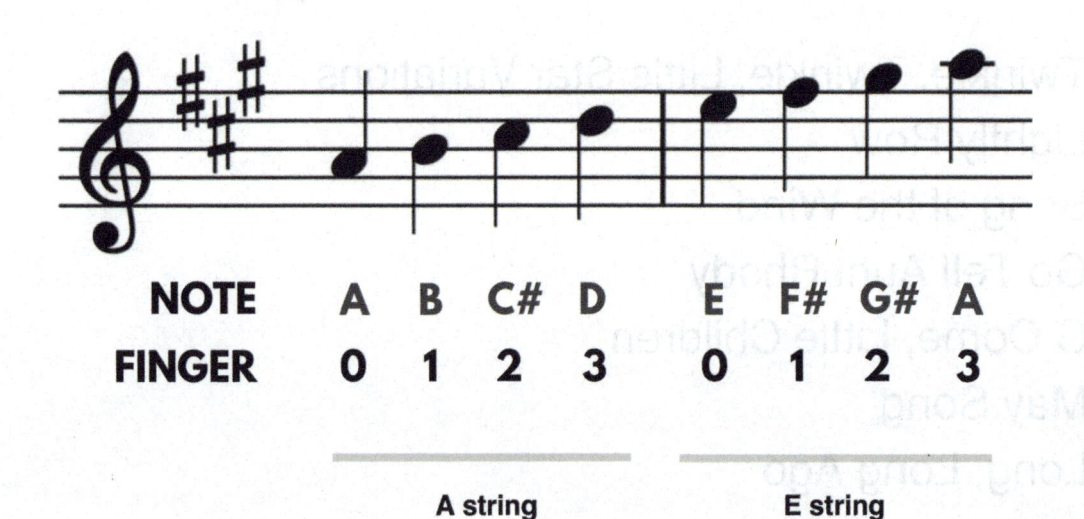

NOTE	A	B	C#	D	E	F#	G#	A
FINGER	0	1	2	3	0	1	2	3

A string   E string

A Major Scale Finger Placement

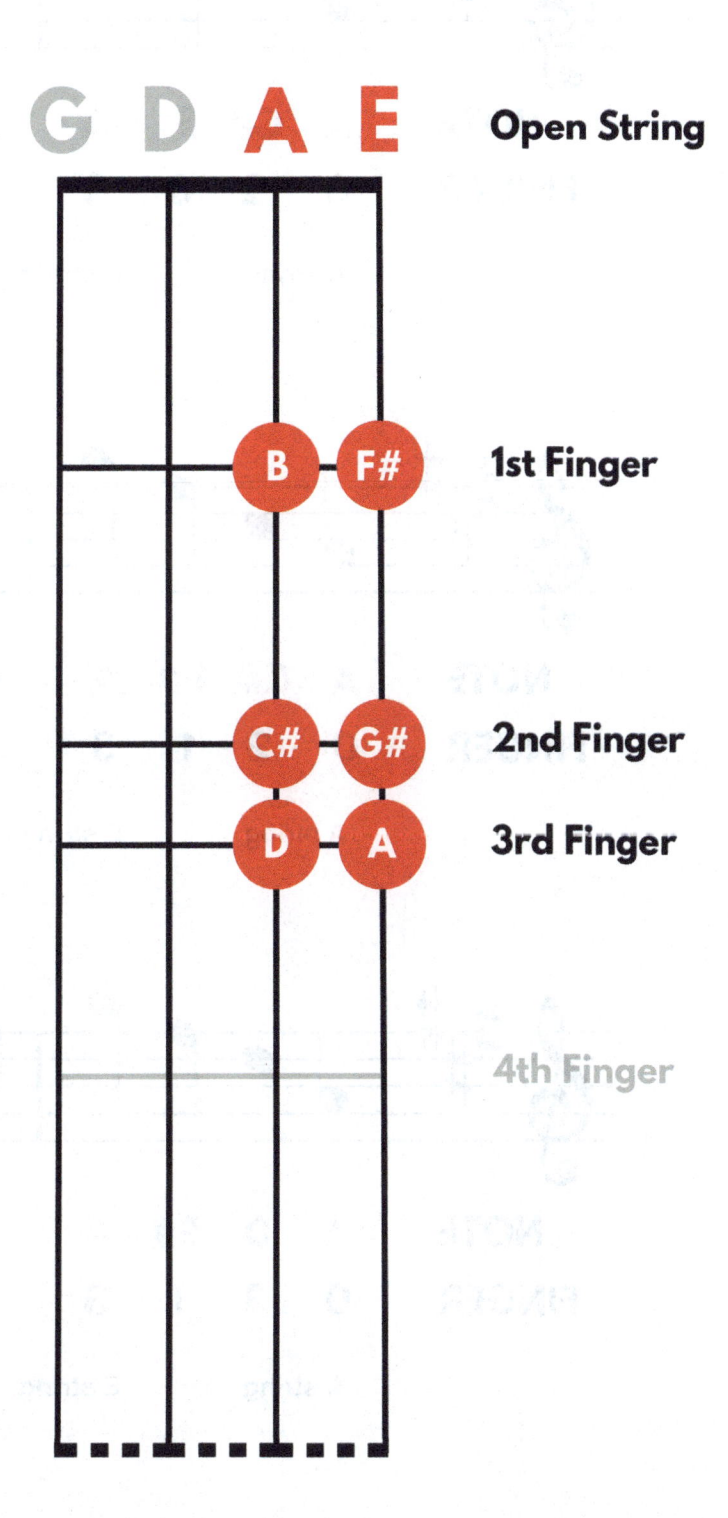

String	G	D	A	E	
					Open String
			B	F#	1st Finger
			C#	G#	2nd Finger
			D	A	3rd Finger
					4th Finger

A Major Arpeggios

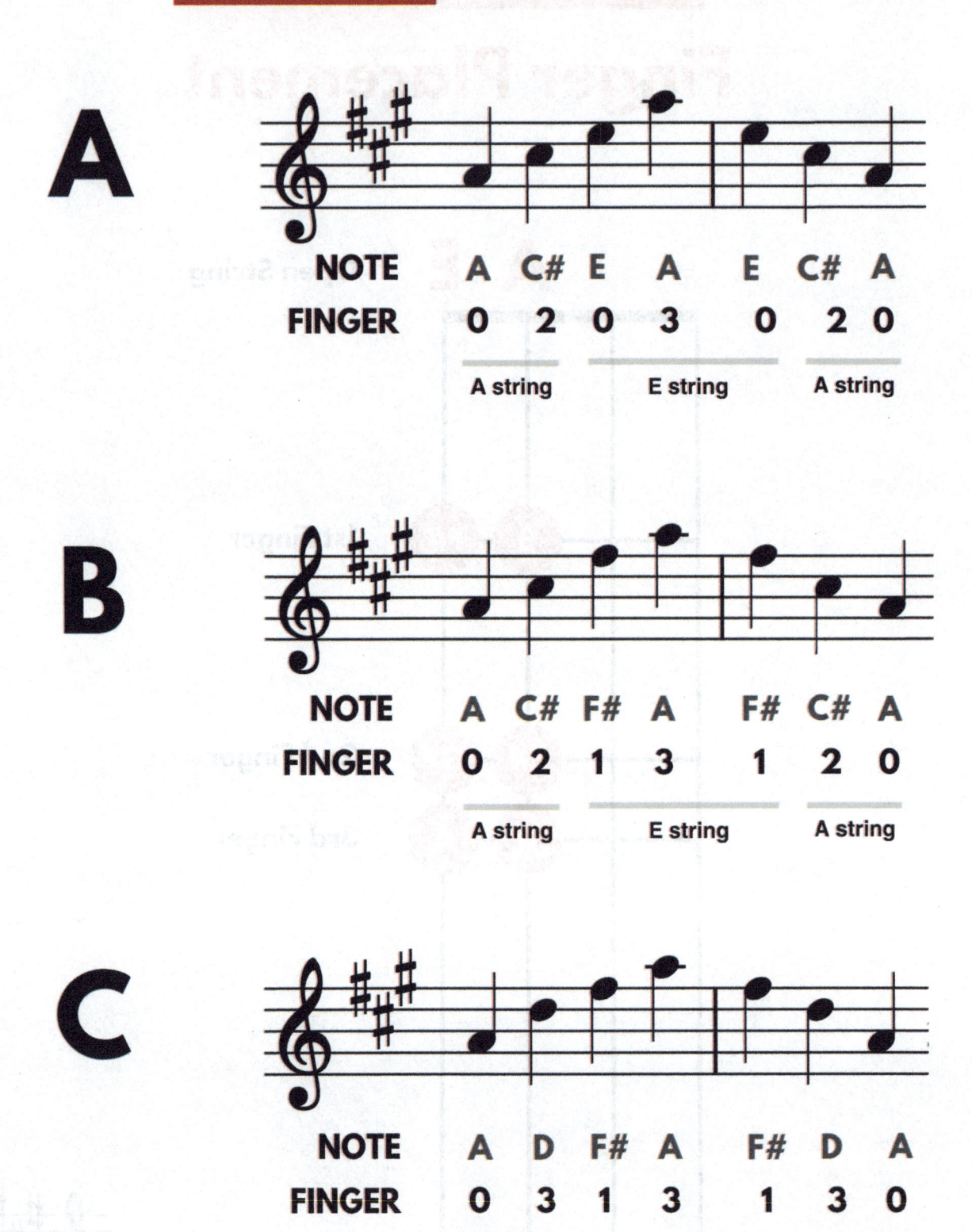

A

NOTE	A	C#	E	A	E	C#	A
FINGER	0	2	0	3	0	2	0

A string — E string — A string

B

NOTE	A	C#	F#	A	F#	C#	A
FINGER	0	2	1	3	1	2	0

A string — E string — A string

C

NOTE	A	D	F#	A	F#	D	A
FINGER	0	3	1	3	1	3	0

A string — E string — A string

A Major Arpeggios Finger Placement

A

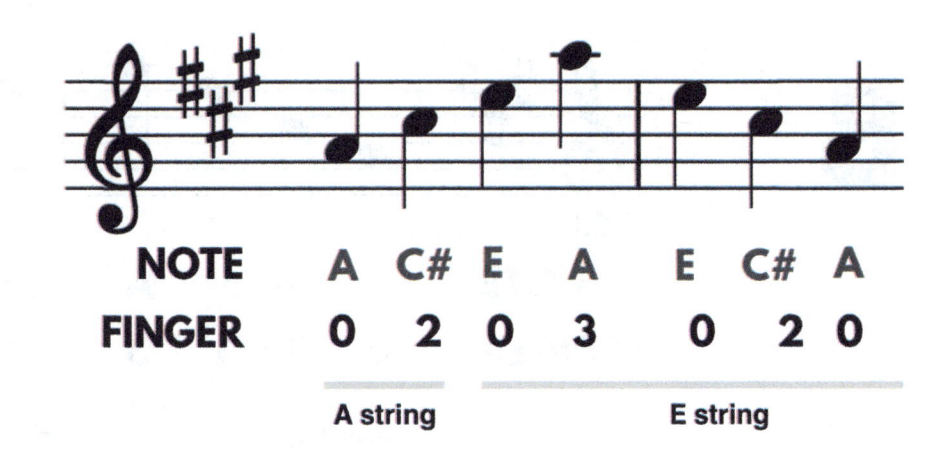

NOTE	A	C#	E	A	E	C#	A
FINGER	0	2	0	3	0	2	0

A string — E string

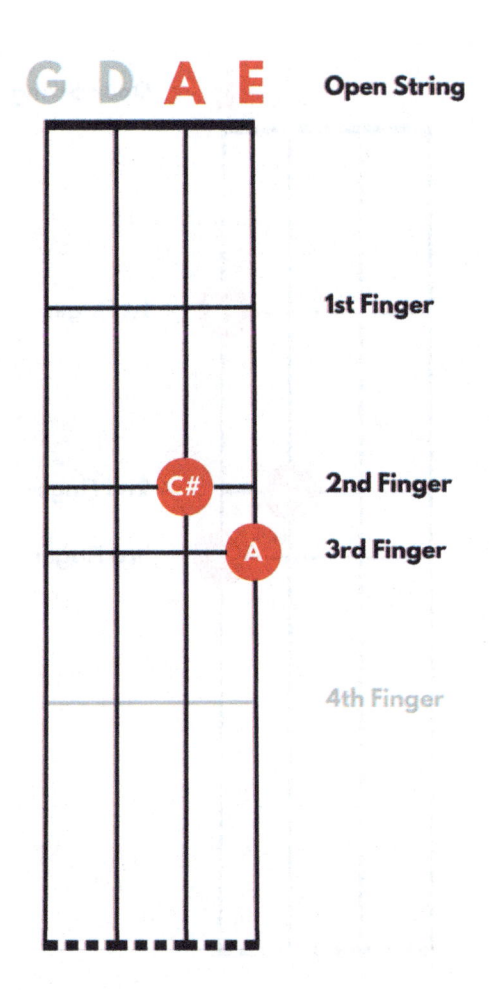

G D **A E** — Open String

1st Finger

C# — 2nd Finger

A — 3rd Finger

4th Finger

50

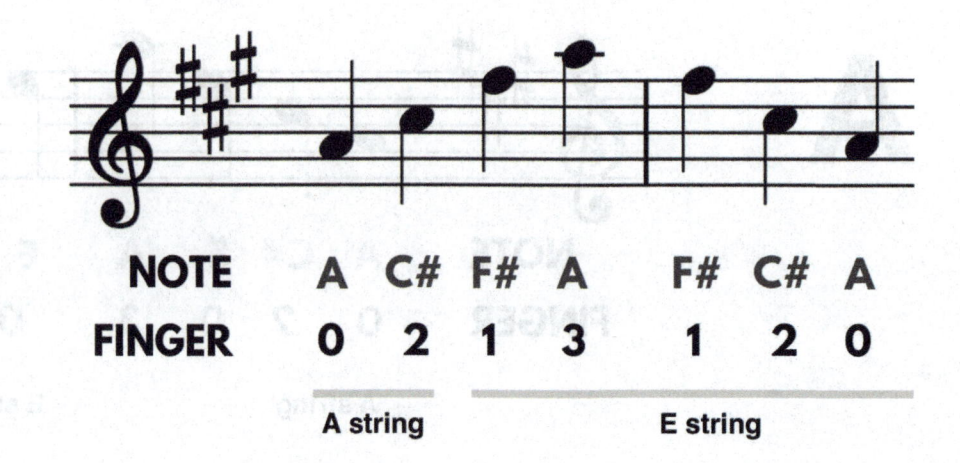

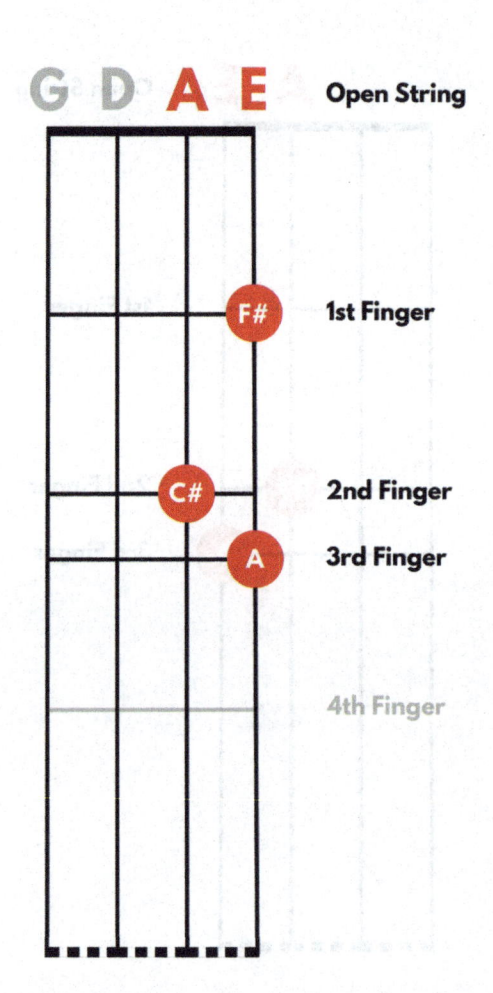

A Major Arpeggios
Finger Placement

B

NOTE	A	C#	F#	A	F#	C#	A
FINGER	0	2	1	3	1	2	0

A string | E string

G D **A E** Open String

F# — 1st Finger

C# — 2nd Finger

A — 3rd Finger

4th Finger

51

A Major Arpeggios
Finger Placement

C

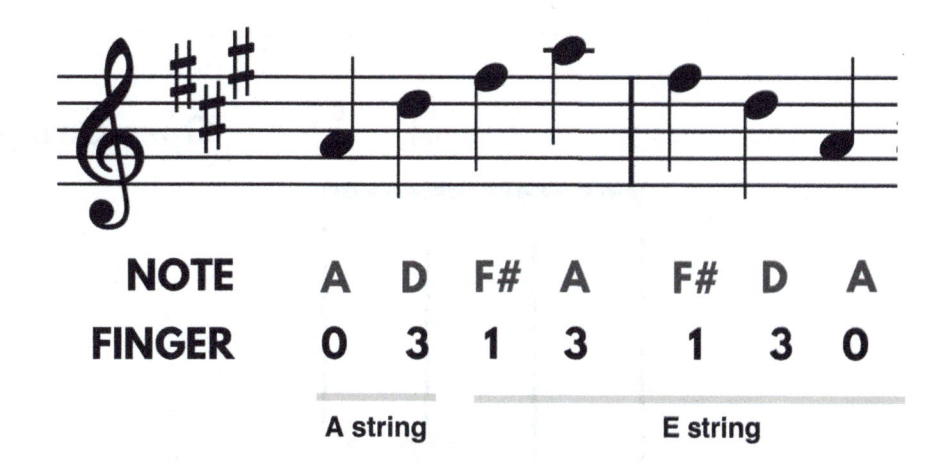

NOTE	A	D	F#	A	F#	D	A
FINGER	0	3	1	3	1	3	0

A string | E string

G D **A E** Open String

F# 1st Finger

2nd Finger

D A 3rd Finger

4th Finger

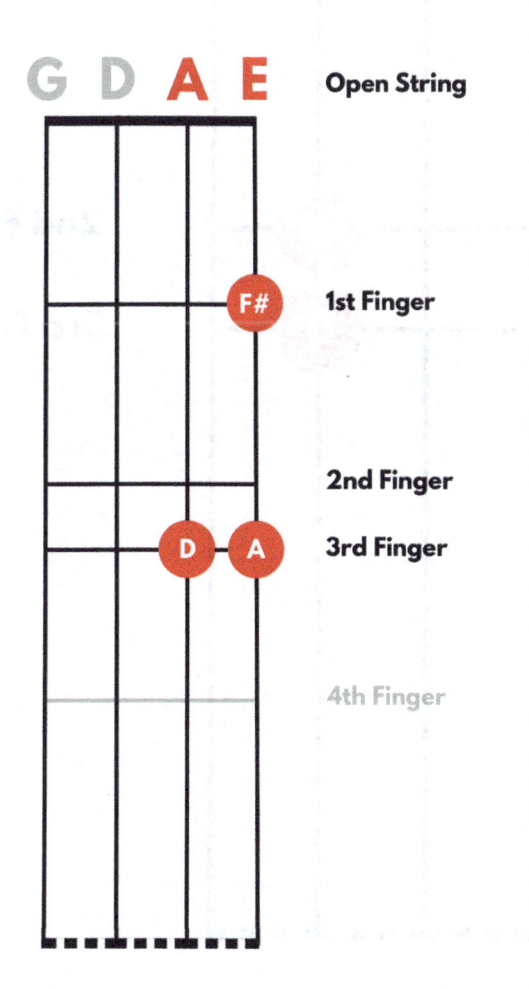

1. Twinkle, Twinkle, Little Star Variations

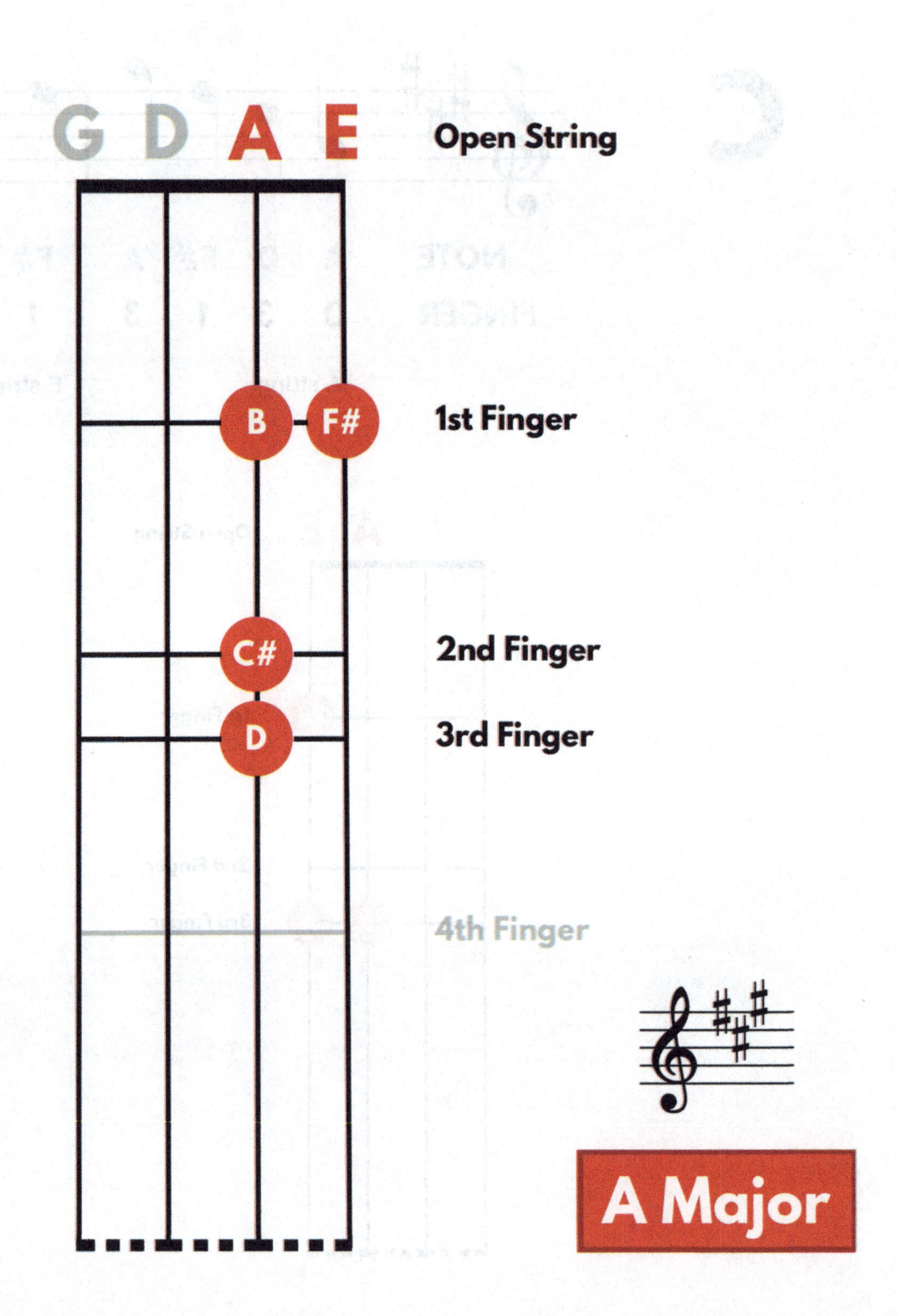

G D A E — Open String

B **F#** — 1st Finger

C# — 2nd Finger

D — 3rd Finger

4th Finger

A Major

2. Lightly Row

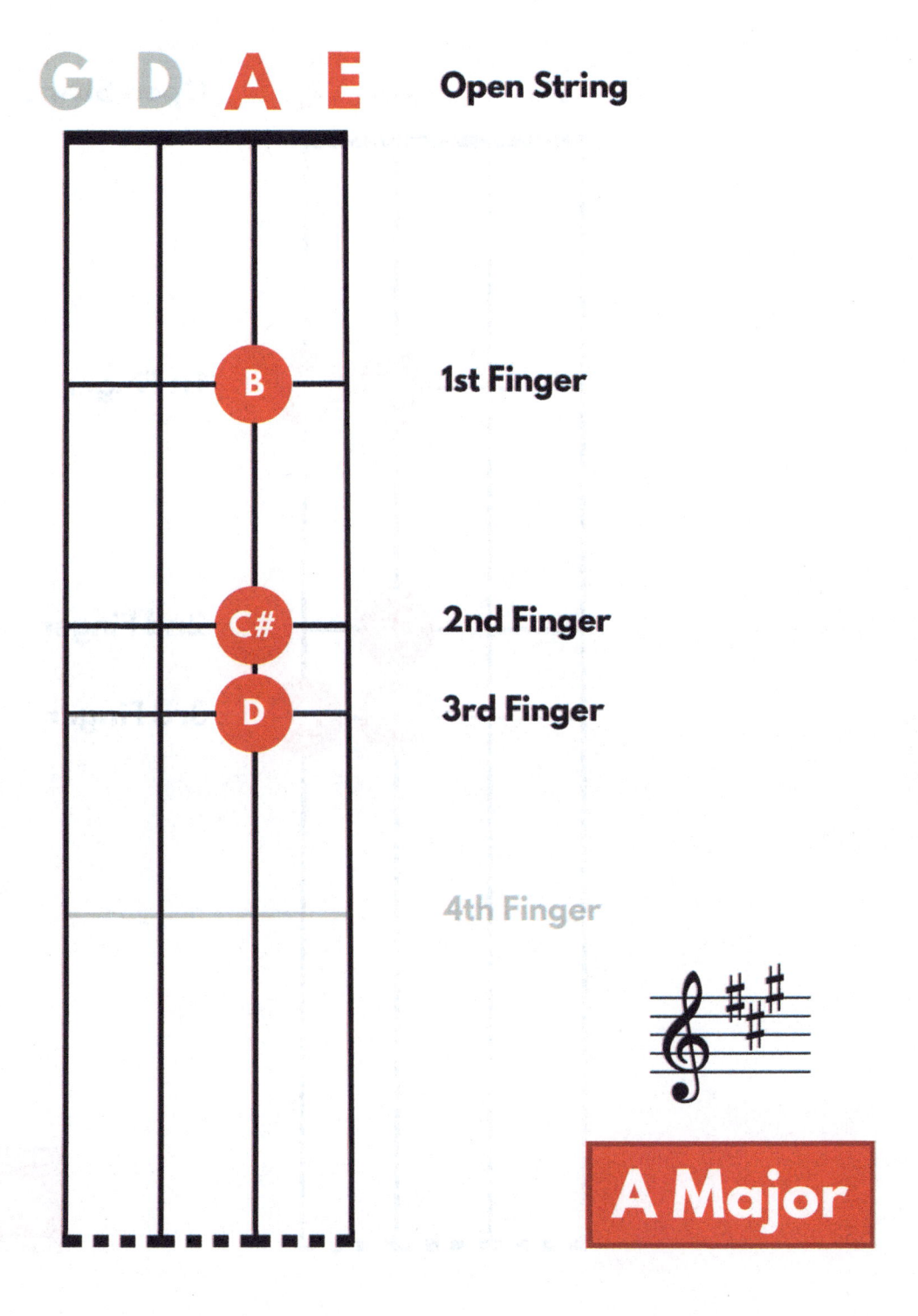

G D A E Open String

B 1st Finger

C# 2nd Finger

D 3rd Finger

4th Finger

A Major

3. Song of the Wind

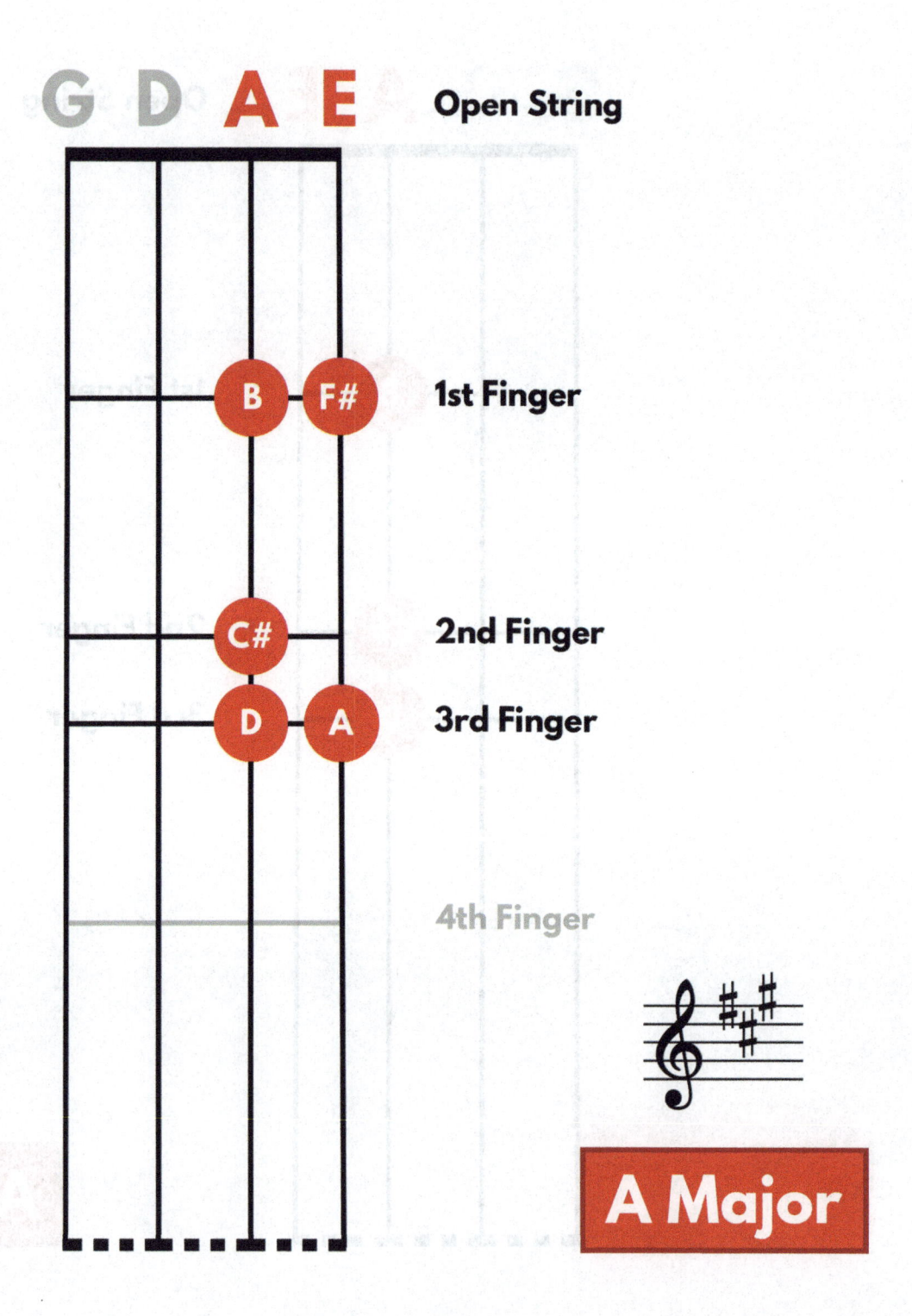

| G | D | **A** | **E** | **Open String** |

B **F#** — 1st Finger

C# — 2nd Finger

D **A** — 3rd Finger

4th Finger

A Major

4. Go Tell Aunt Rhody

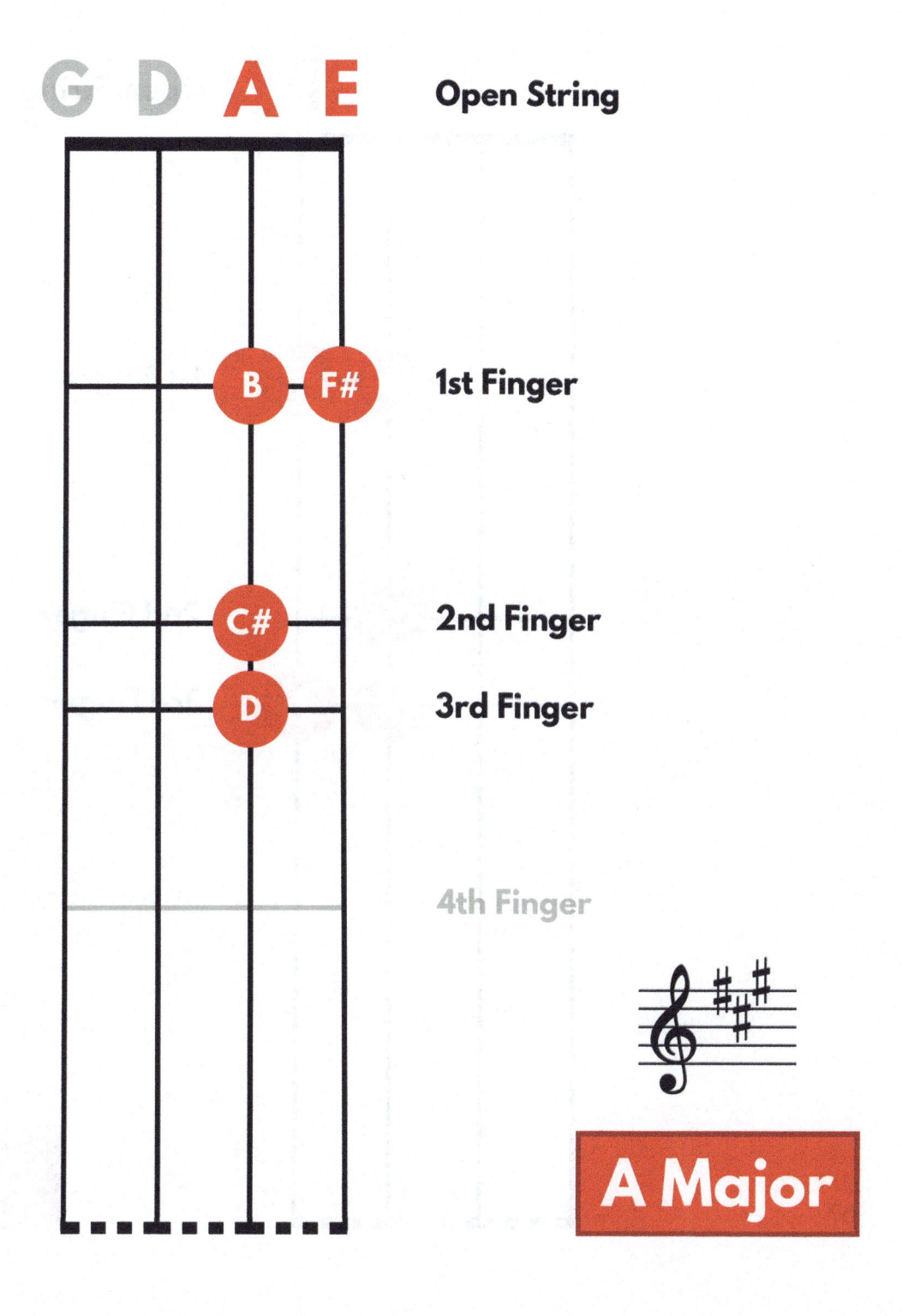

G D A E   **Open String**

B F#   **1st Finger**

C#   **2nd Finger**

D   **3rd Finger**

4th Finger

A Major

5. O Come, Little Children

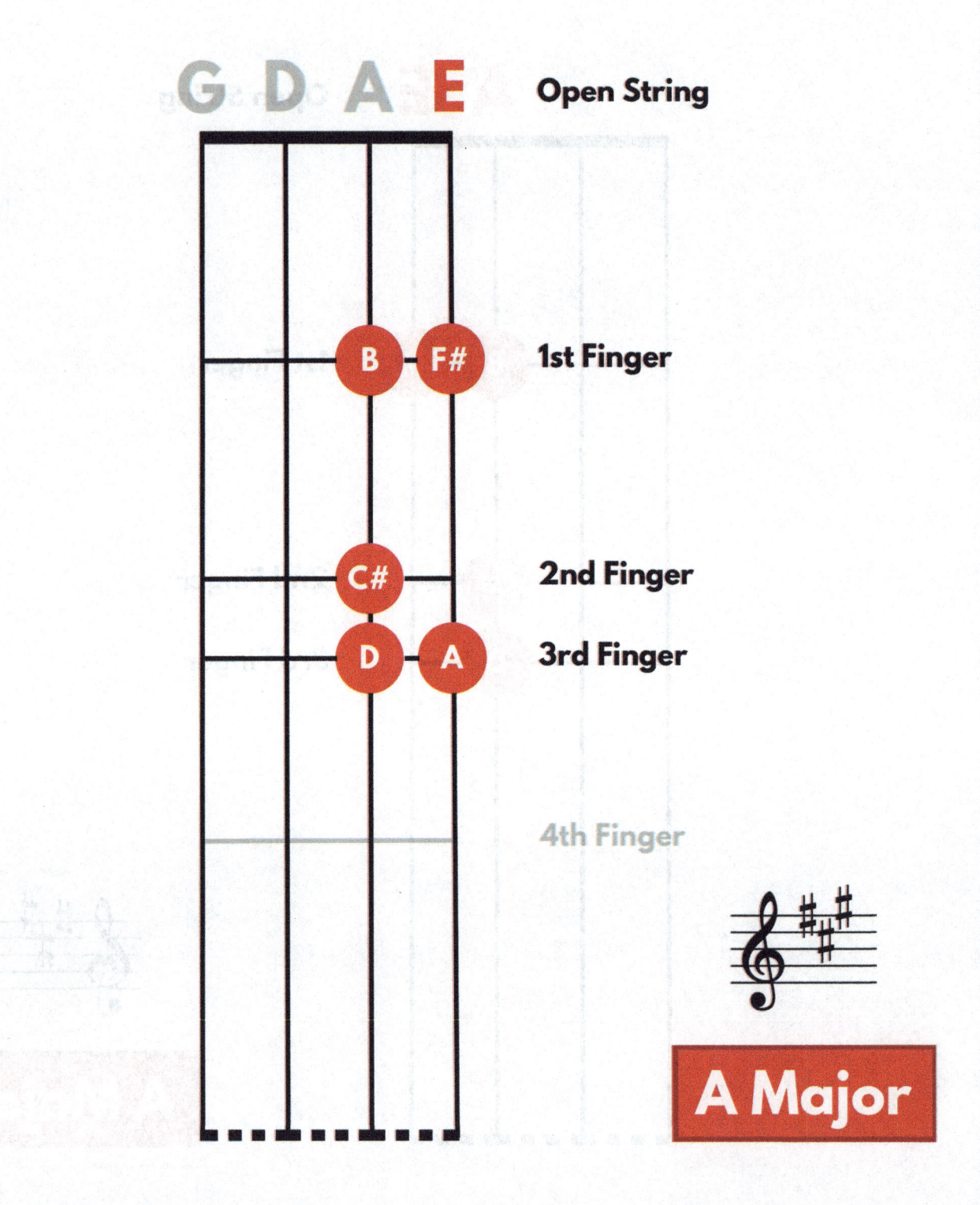

G D A E — Open String

B, F# — 1st Finger

C# — 2nd Finger

D, A — 3rd Finger

4th Finger

A Major

6. May Song

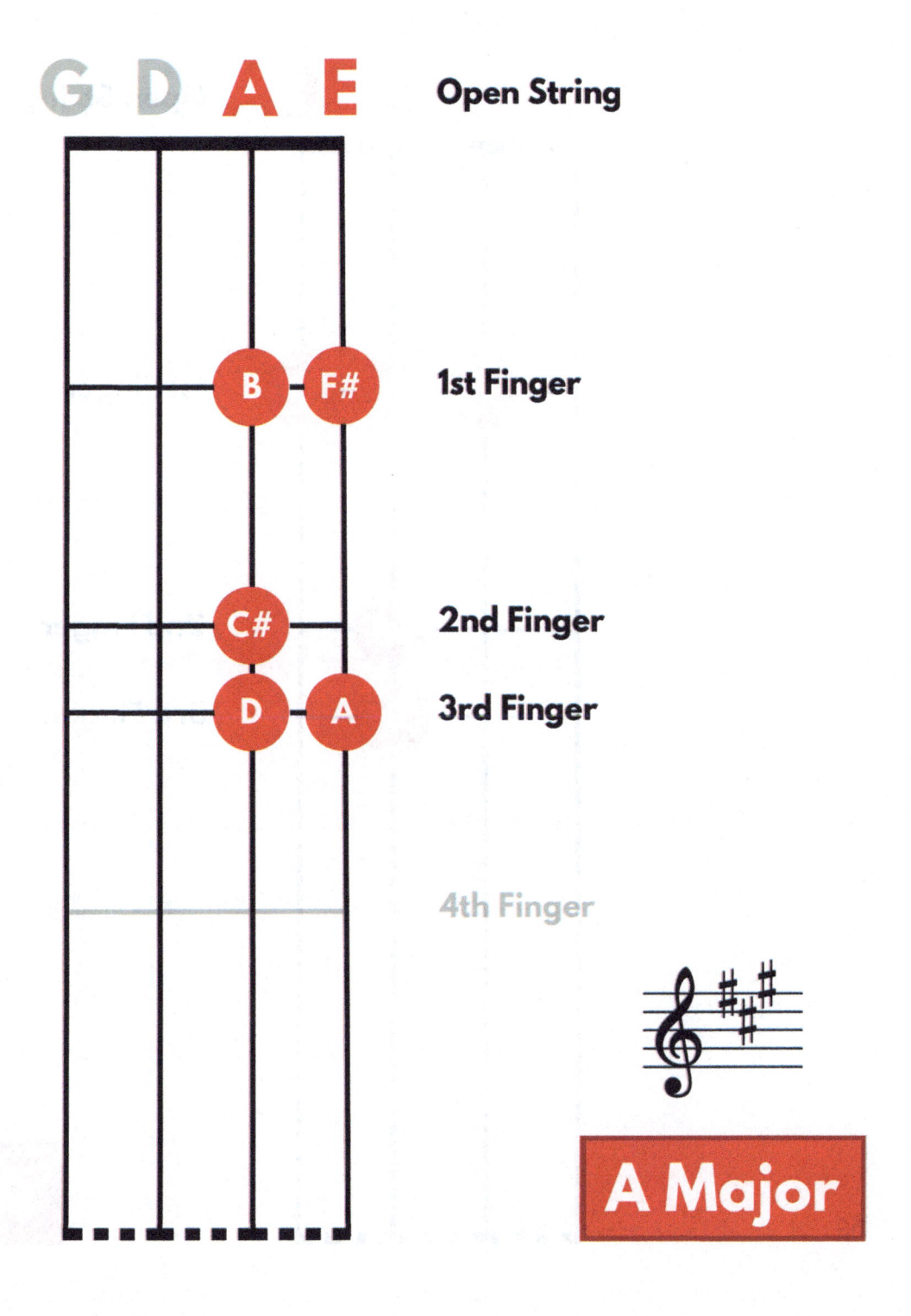

String	G	D	A	E
Open String				
1st Finger			B	F#
2nd Finger			C#	
3rd Finger			D	A
4th Finger				

A Major

7. Long, Long Ago

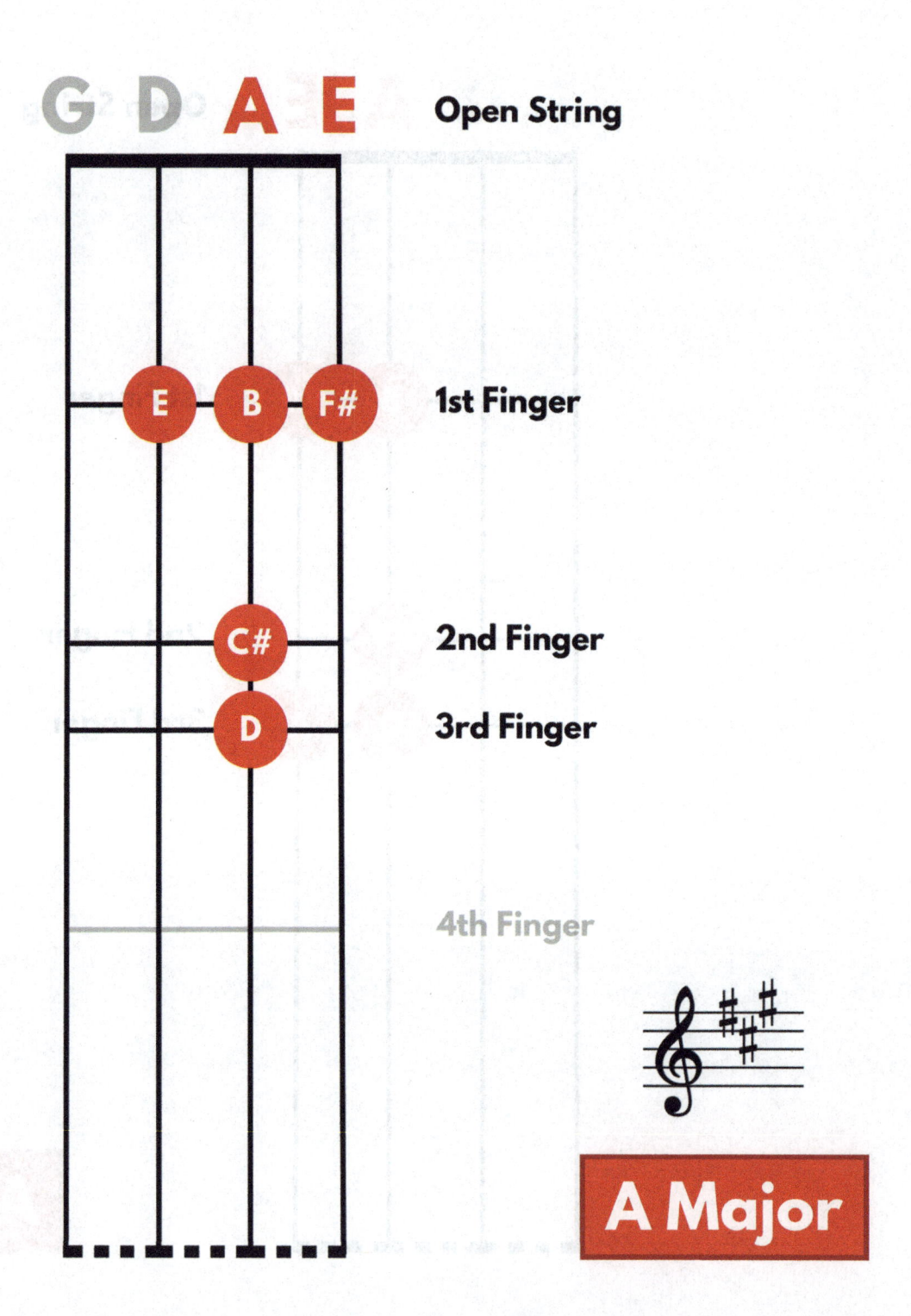

G D A E Open String

E B F# 1st Finger

C# 2nd Finger

D 3rd Finger

4th Finger

A Major

59

8. Allegro

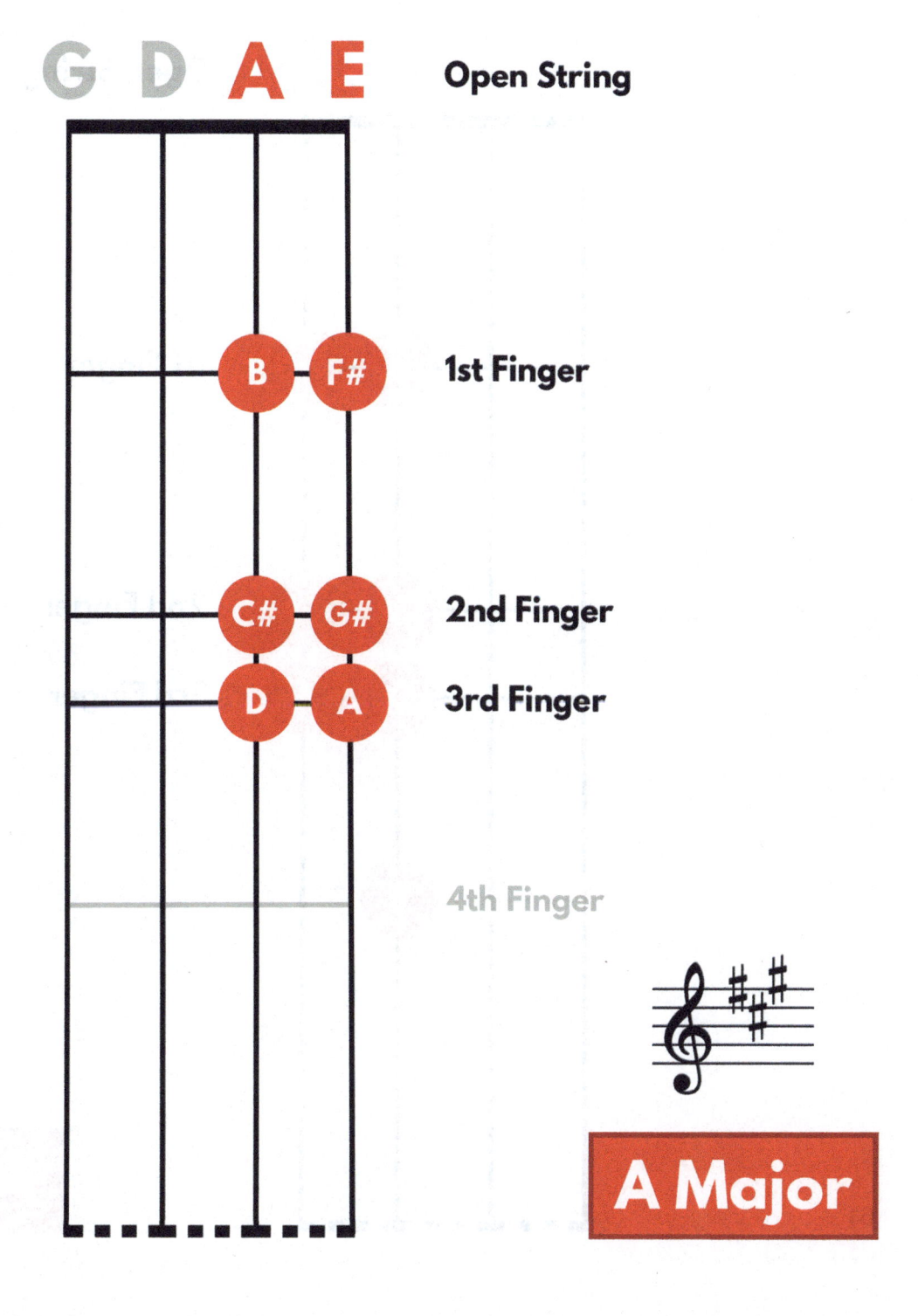

G D A E Open String

B F# 1st Finger

C# G# 2nd Finger

D A 3rd Finger

4th Finger

A Major

9. Perpetual Motion

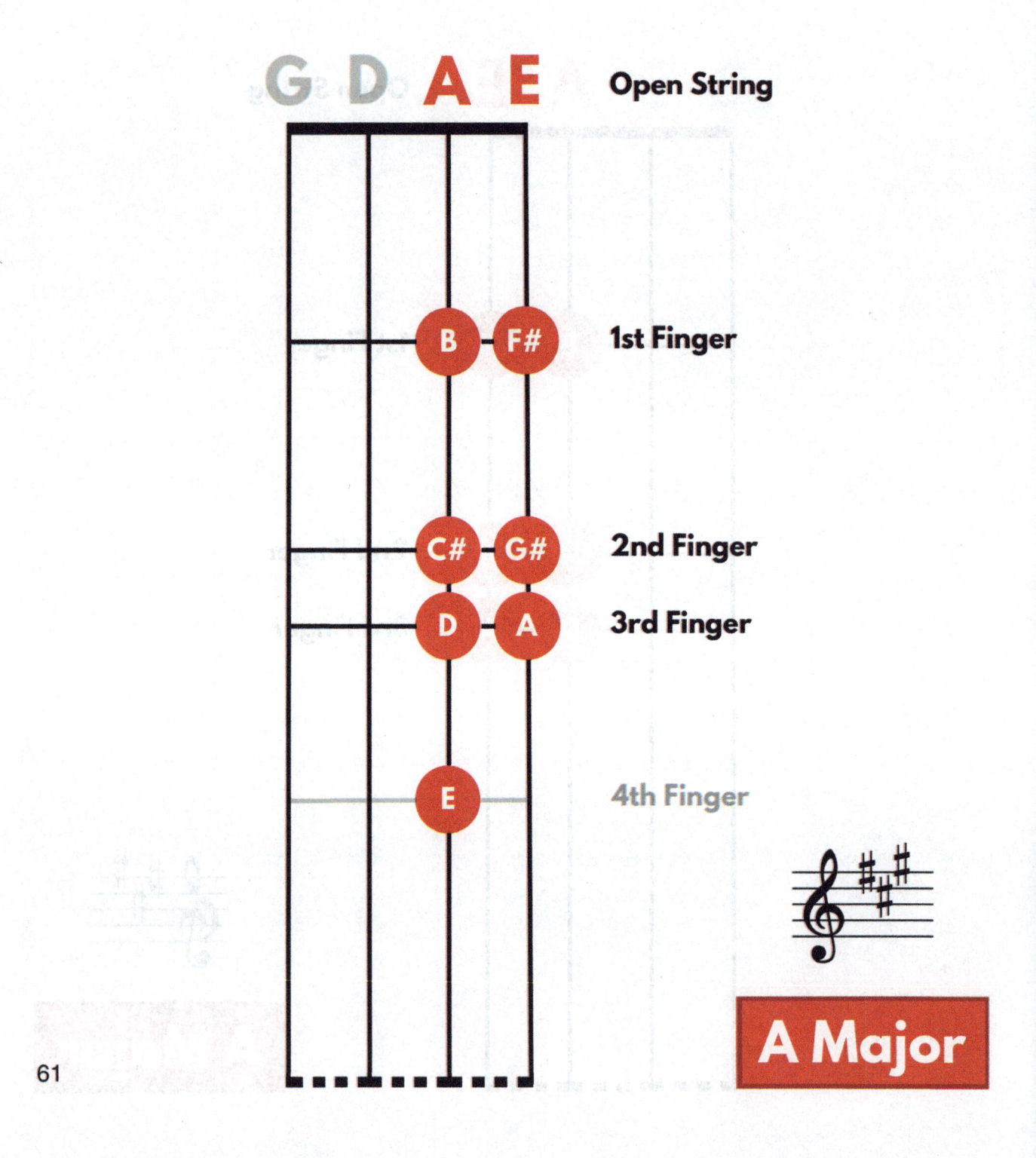

G D A E   Open String

B **F#**   1st Finger

C# **G#**   2nd Finger

D **A**   3rd Finger

E   4th Finger

A Major

D Major

D Major

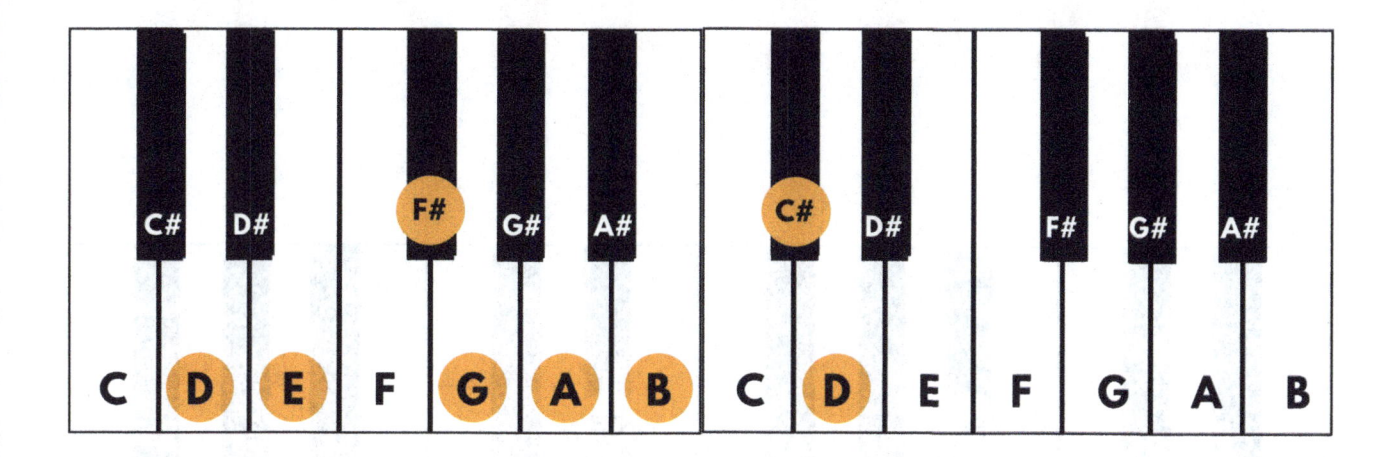

D E F# G A B C# D

W W H W W W H

Pieces in Book 1 in D Major:

10. Allegretto
11. Andantino

D Major Scale

D E F# G A B C# D

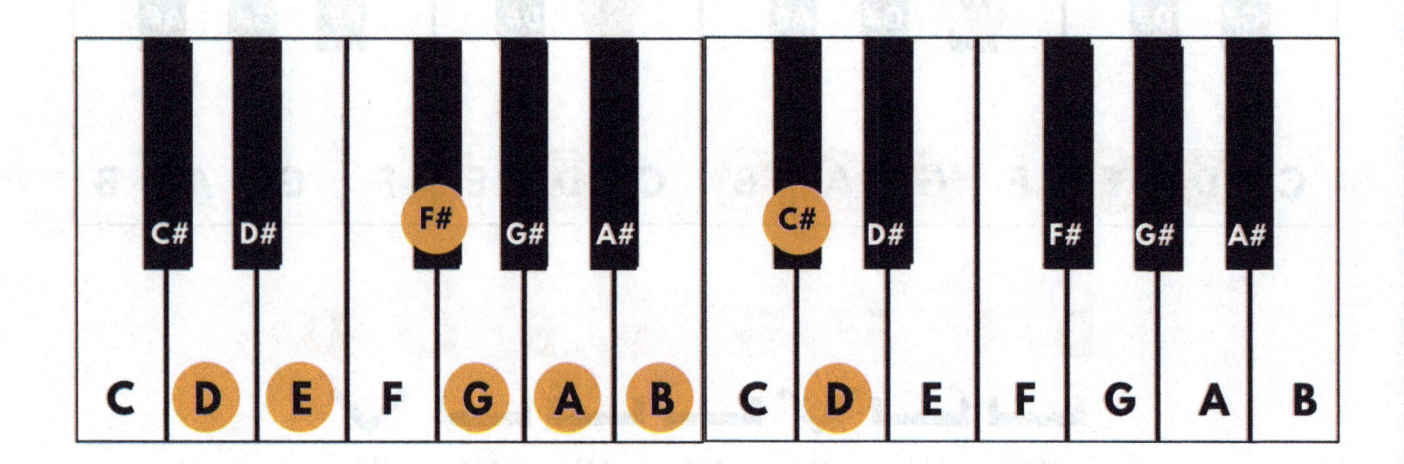

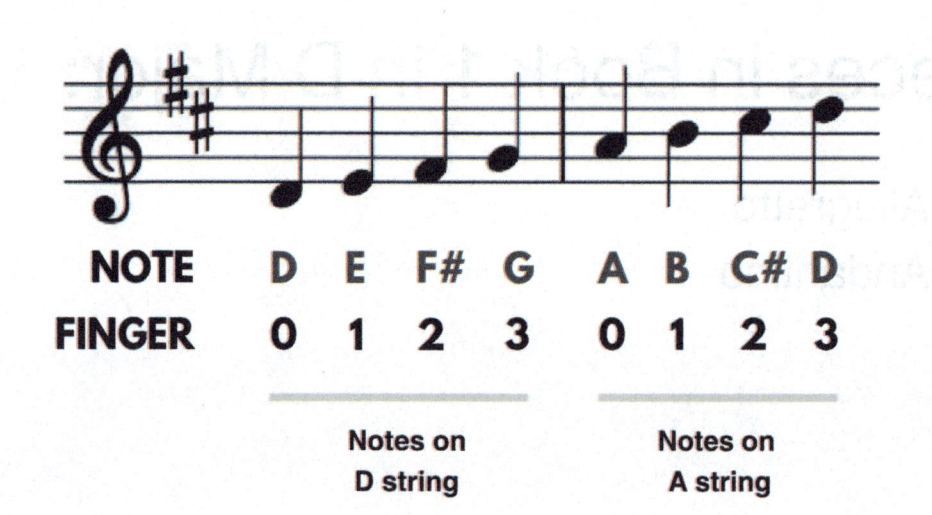

NOTE	D	E	F#	G	A	B	C#	D
FINGER	0	1	2	3	0	1	2	3

Notes on D string · Notes on A string

D Major Scale
Finger Placement

String	Position
G D A E	Open String
E, B (on D and A)	1st Finger
F#, C# (on D and A)	2nd Finger
G, D (on D and A)	3rd Finger
	4th Finger

D Major Arpeggios

A

NOTE	D	F#	A	D	A	F#	D
FINGER	0	2	0	3	0	2	0

D string — A string — D string

B

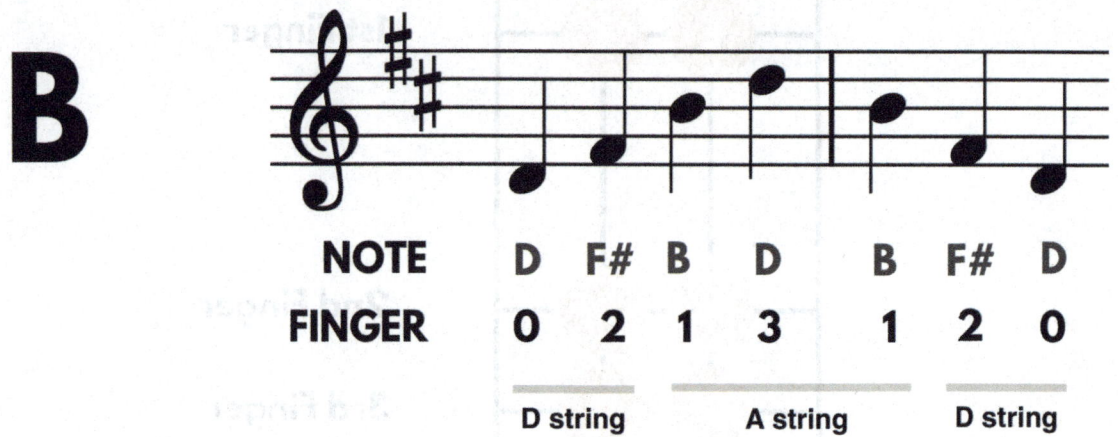

NOTE	D	F#	B	D	B	F#	D
FINGER	0	2	1	3	1	2	0

D string — A string — D string

C

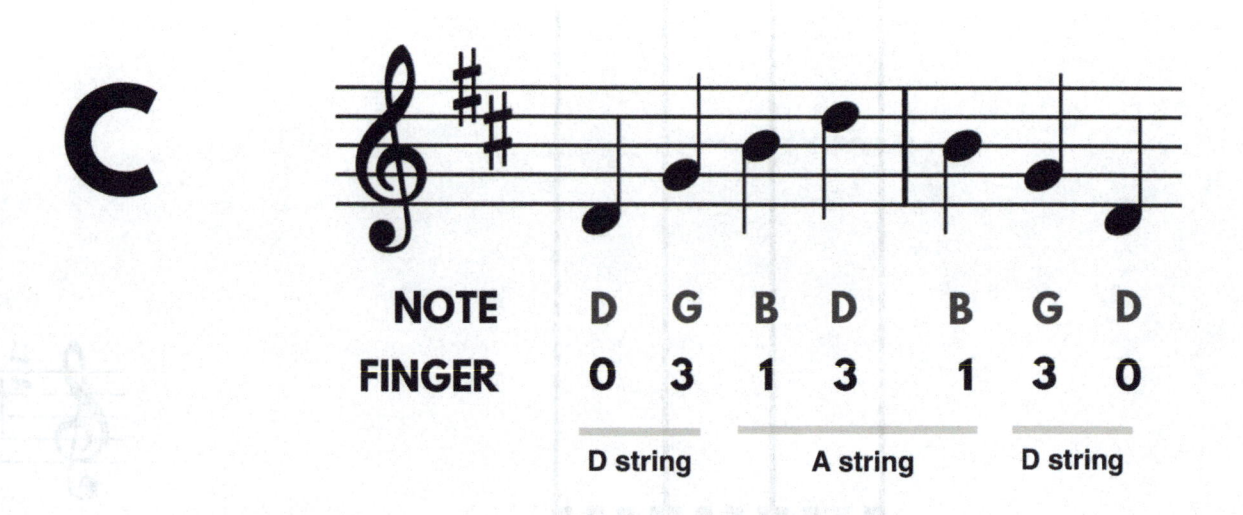

NOTE	D	G	B	D	B	G	D
FINGER	0	3	1	3	1	3	0

D string — A string — D string

D Major Arpeggios
Finger Placement

A

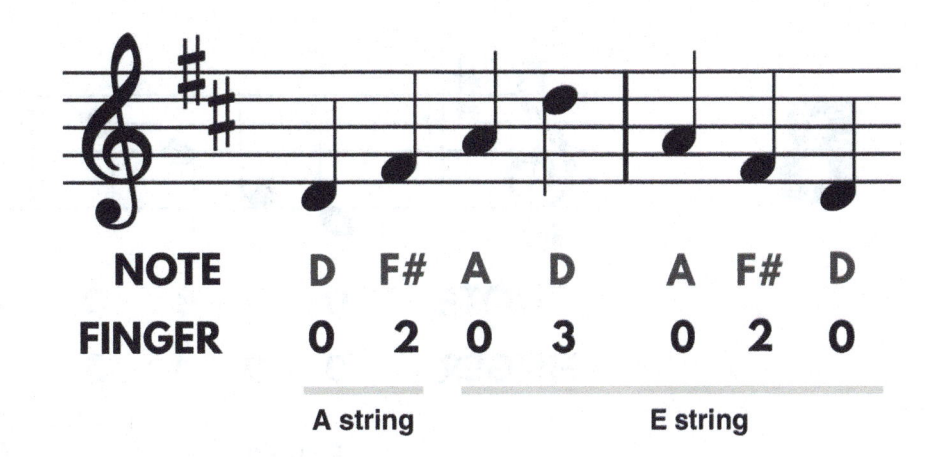

NOTE	D	F#	A	D	A	F#	D
FINGER	0	2	0	3	0	2	0

A string | E string

G D A E Open String

1st Finger

F# — 2nd Finger

D — 3rd Finger

4th Finger

68

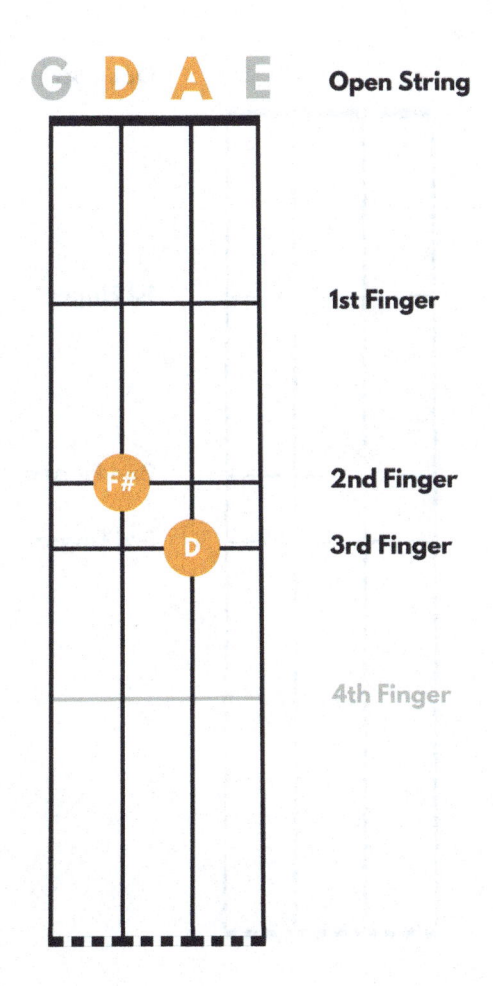

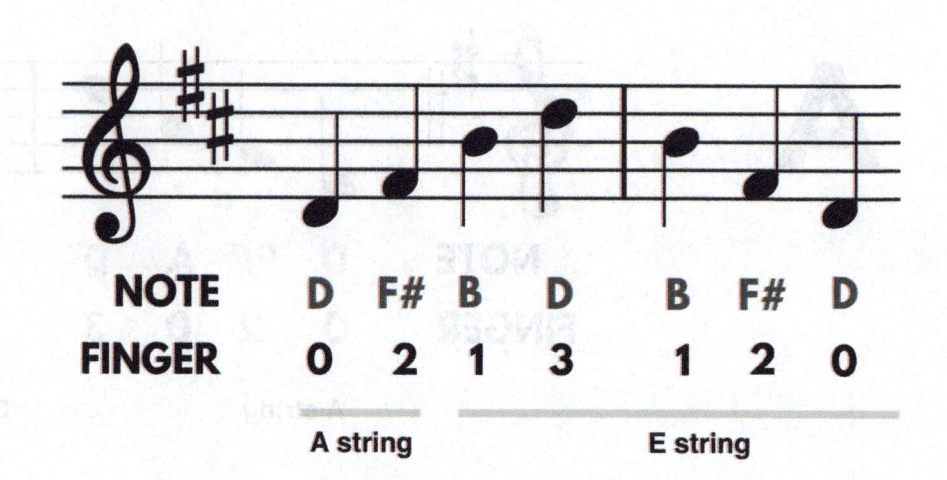

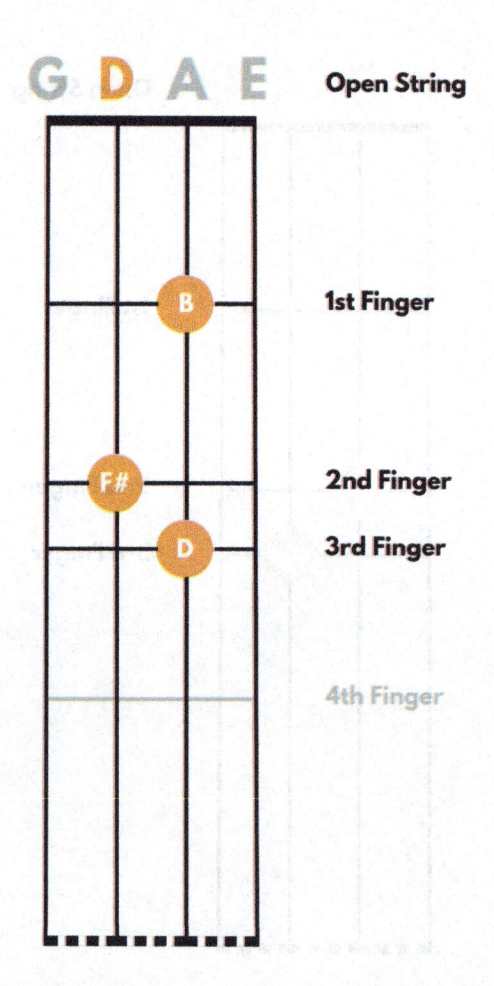

D Major Arpeggios
Finger Placement

B

NOTE	D	F#	B	D	B	F#	D
FINGER	0	2	1	3	1	2	0

A string | E string

G D A E Open String

- B — 1st Finger
- F# — 2nd Finger
- D — 3rd Finger
- 4th Finger

69

D Major Arpeggios
Finger Placement

C

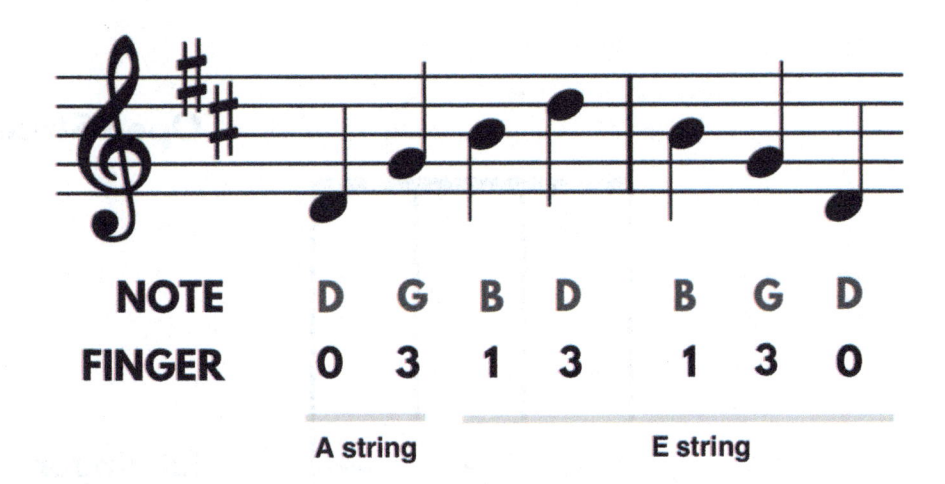

NOTE	D	G	B	D	B	G	D
FINGER	0	3	1	3	1	3	0

A string | E string

G D A E Open String

1st Finger — B

2nd Finger

3rd Finger — G, D

4th Finger

70

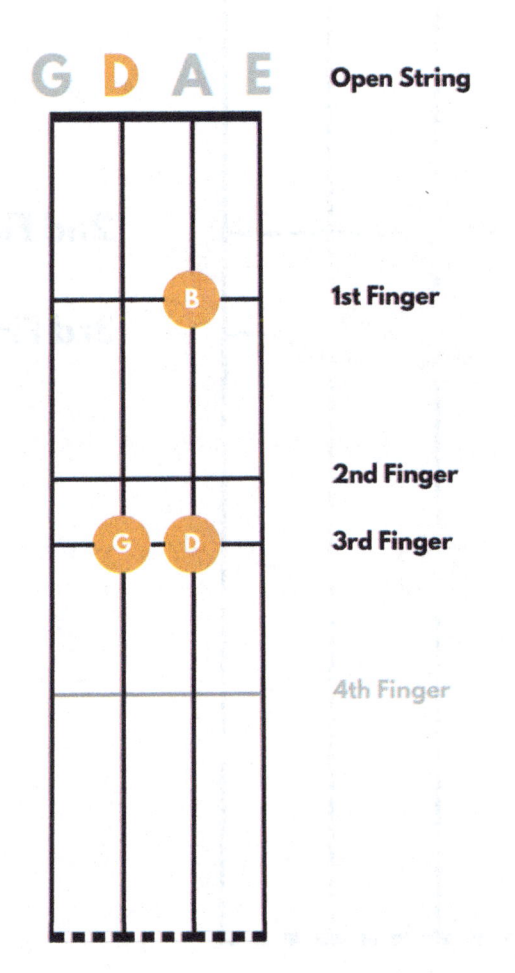

10. Allegretto

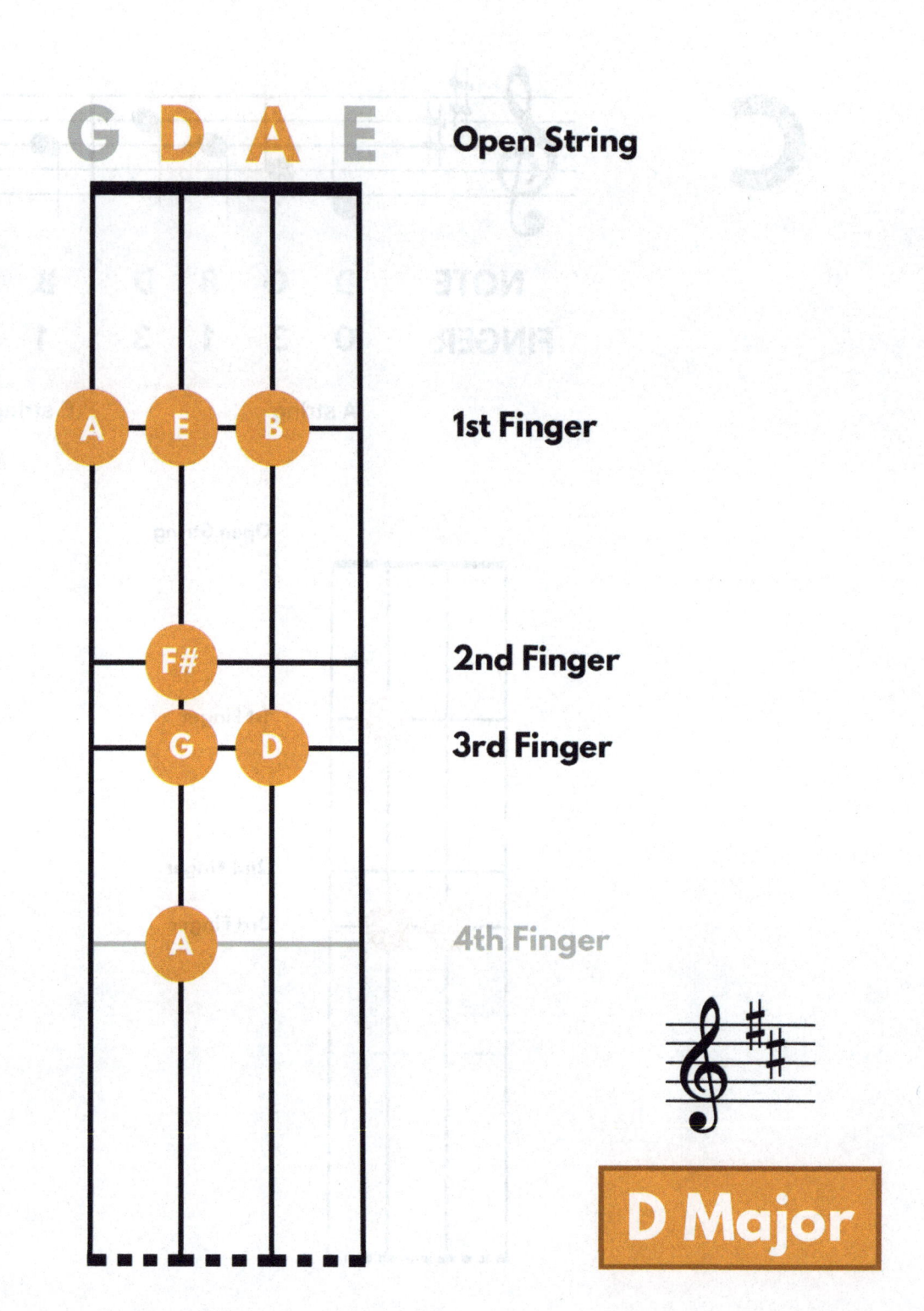

G D A E Open String

A E B 1st Finger

F# 2nd Finger

G D 3rd Finger

A 4th Finger

D Major

71

11. Andantino

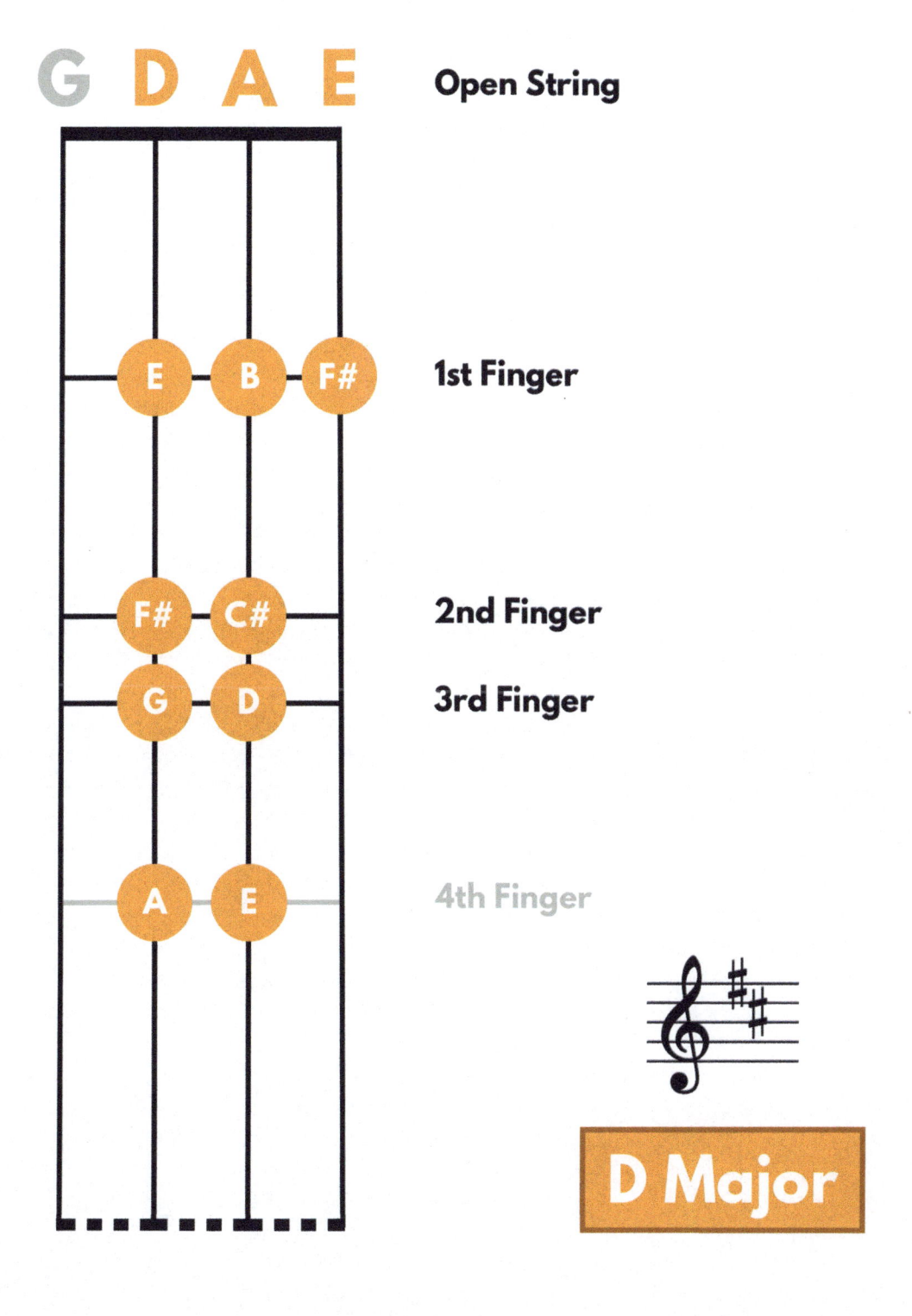

Open String: G D A E

1st Finger: E B F#

2nd Finger: F# C#

3rd Finger: G D

4th Finger: A E

D Major

G Major

G Major

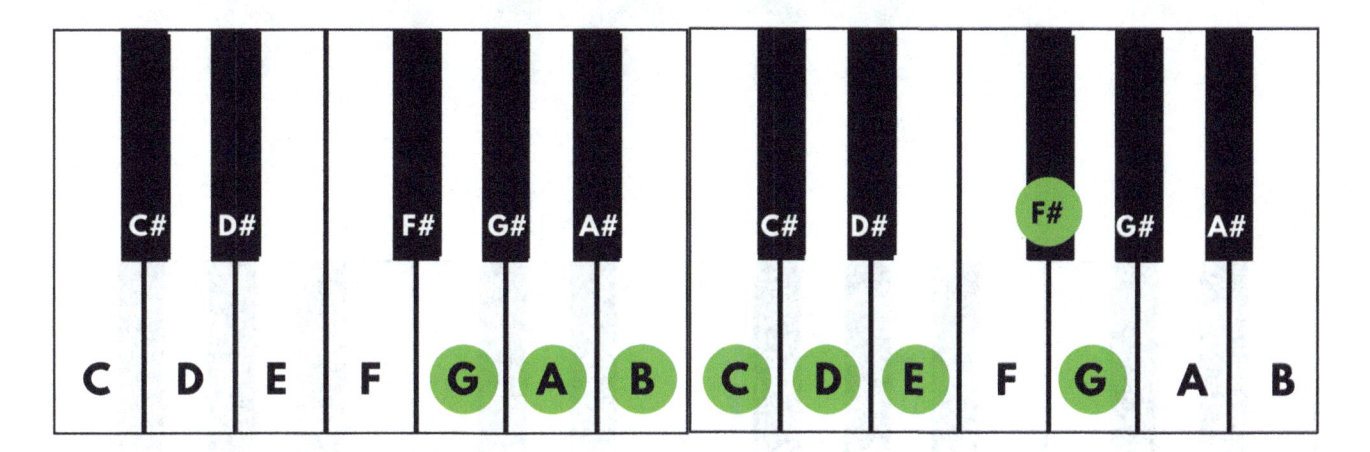

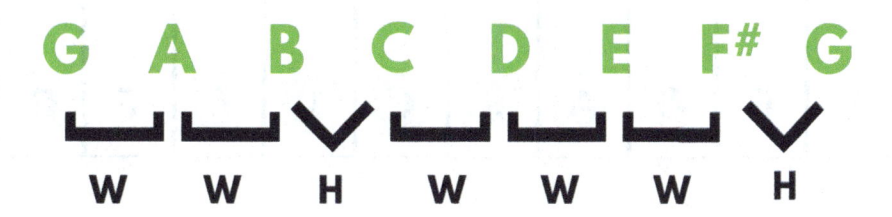

G A B C D E F# G

W W H W W W H

Pieces in Book 1 in G Major:

12. Etude
13. Minuet 1
14. Minuet 2
15. Minuet 3
16. The Happy Farmer
17. Gossec Gavotte

G Major Scale

G A B C D E F# G

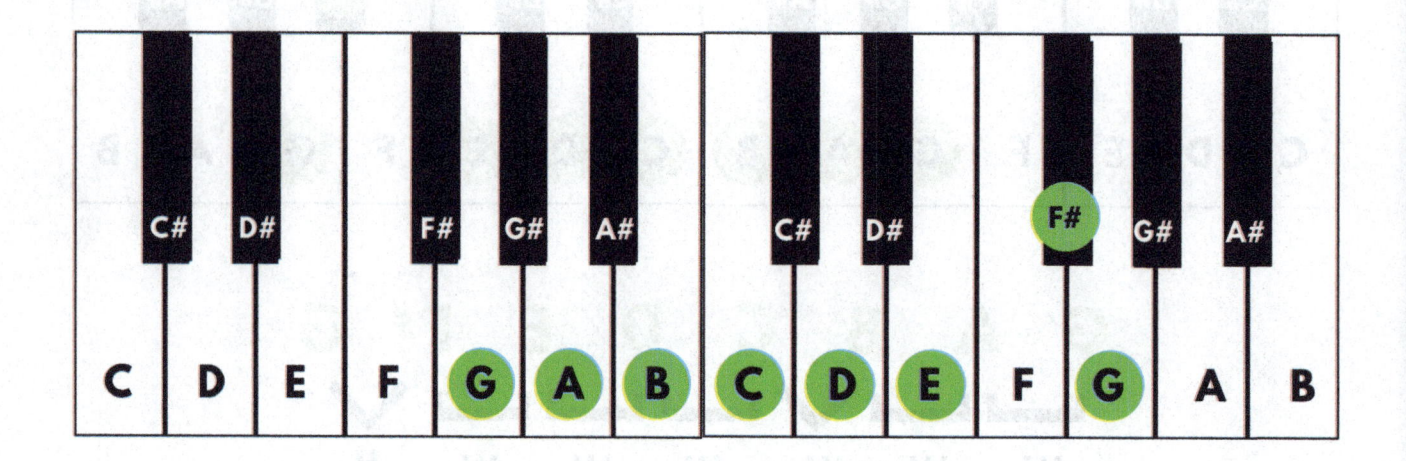

NOTE	G	A	B	C	D	E	F#	G	A	B	C	D	E	F#	G
FINGER	0	1	2	3	0	1	2	3	0	1	2	3	0	1	2

Notes on G string   Notes on D string   Notes on A string   Notes on E string

77

G Major Scale
Finger Placement

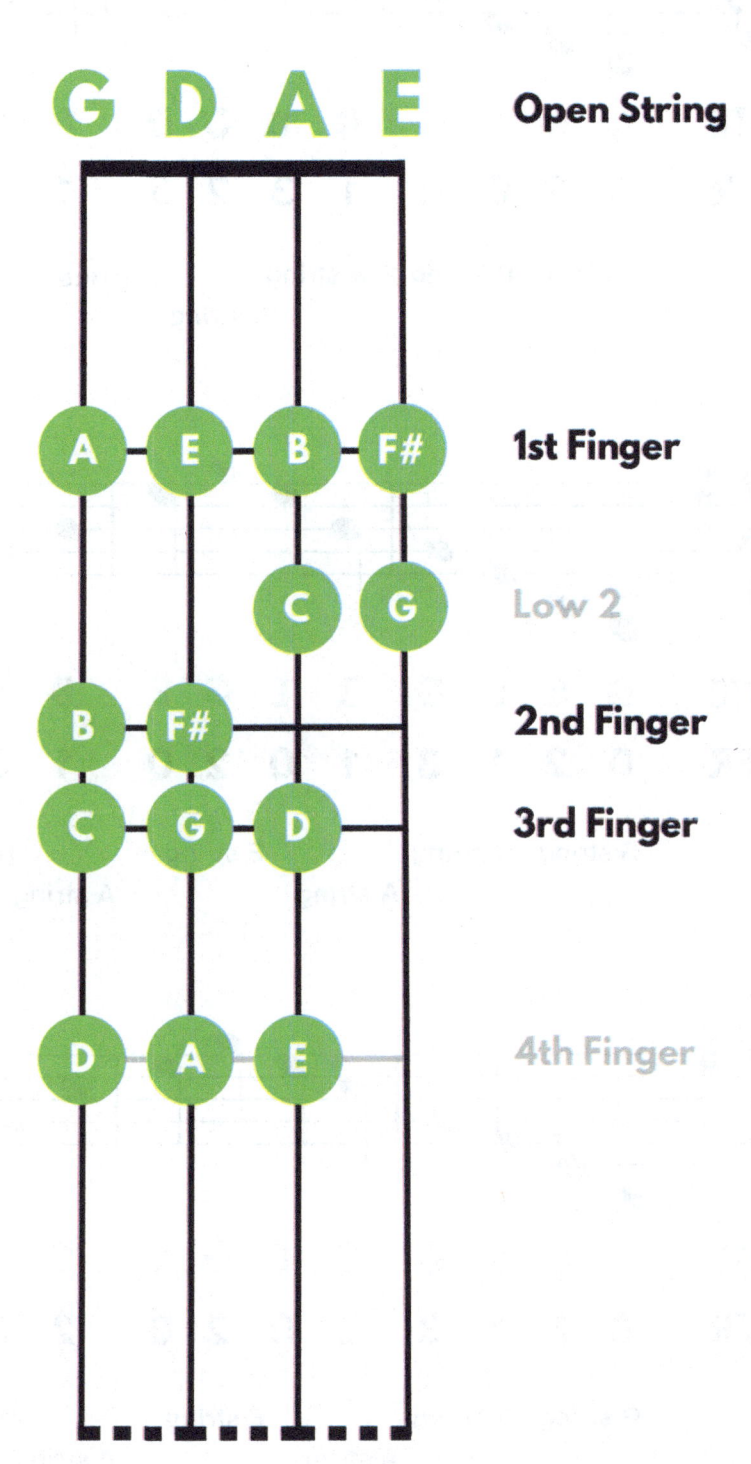

G	D	A	E		Open String
A	E	B	F#		1st Finger
		C	G		Low 2
B	F#				2nd Finger
C	G	D			3rd Finger
D	A	E			4th Finger

G Major Arpeggios

A

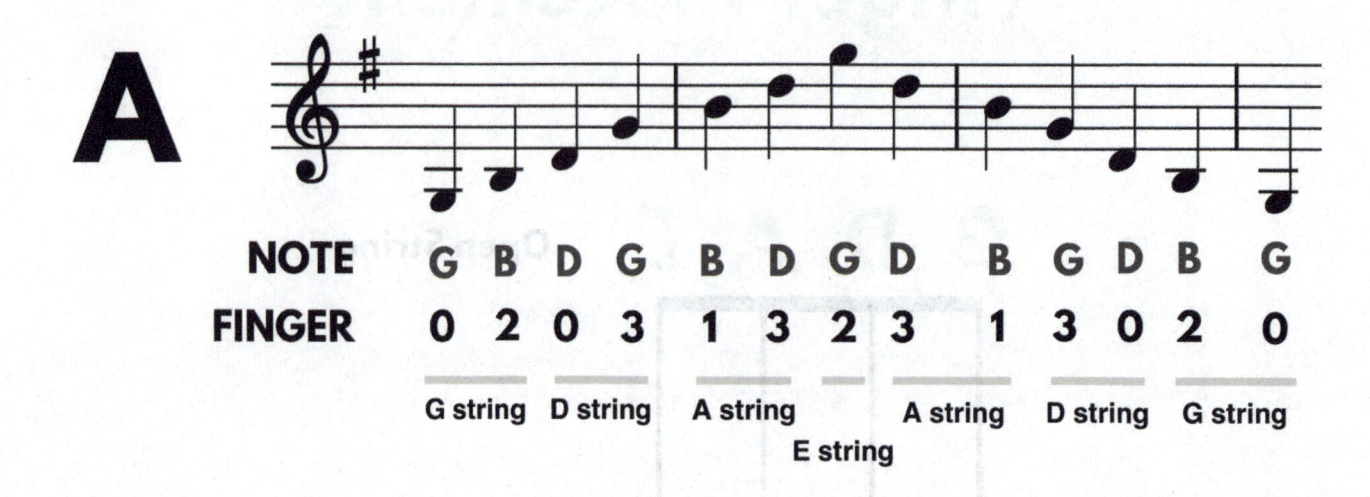

NOTE	G	B	D	G	B	D	G	D	B	G	D	B	G
FINGER	0	2	0	3	1	3	2	3	1	3	0	2	0

G string — D string — A string — E string — A string — D string — G string

B

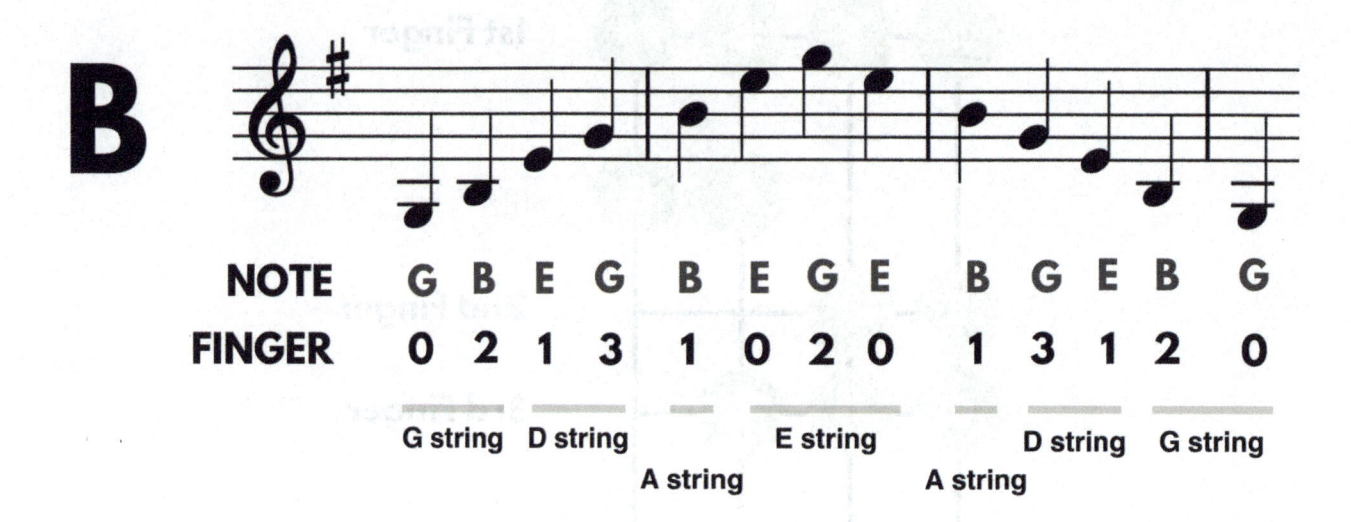

NOTE	G	B	E	G	B	E	G	E	B	G	E	B	G
FINGER	0	2	1	3	1	0	2	0	3	1	2	0	—

G string — D string — A string — E string — A string — D string — G string

C

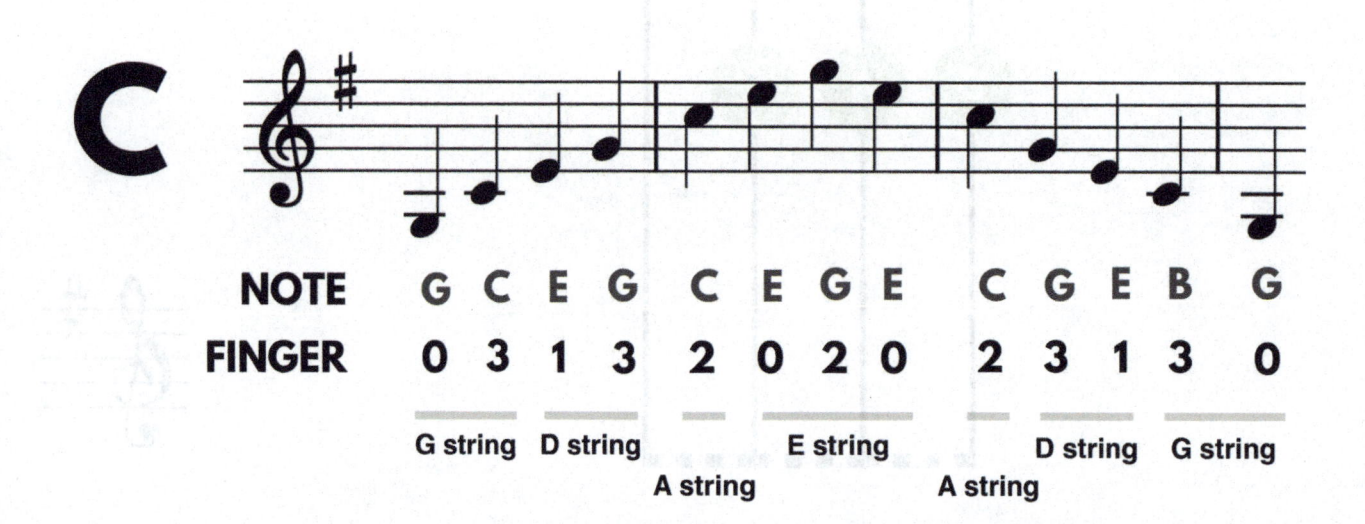

NOTE	G	C	E	G	C	E	G	E	C	G	E	B	G
FINGER	0	3	1	3	2	0	2	0	2	3	1	3	0

G string — D string — A string — E string — A string — D string — G string

G Major Arpeggios
Finger Placement

A

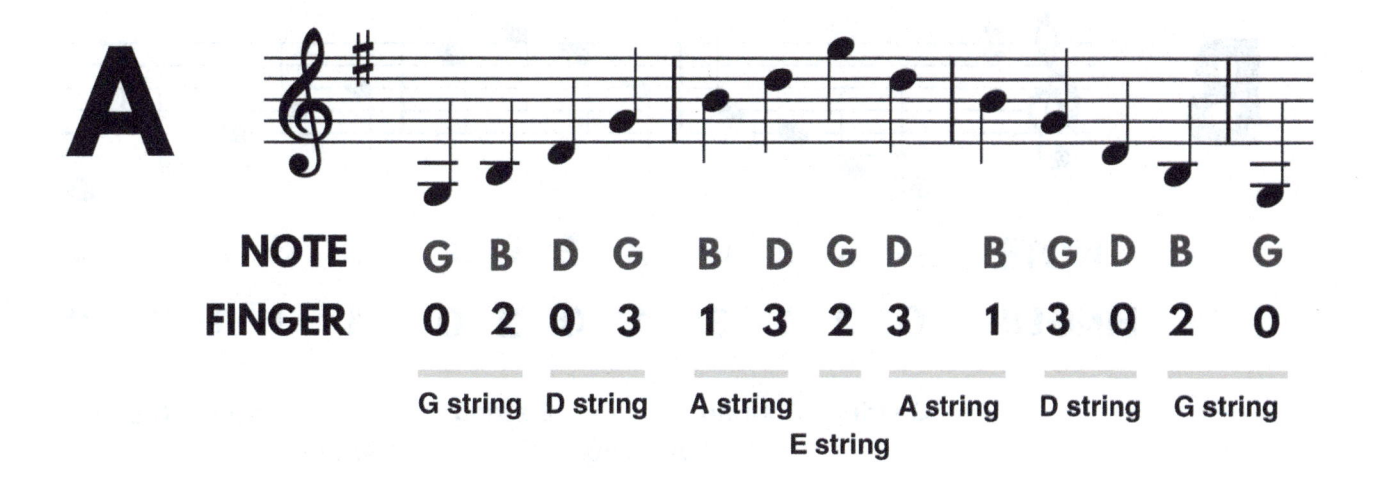

NOTE	G	B	D	G	B	D	G	D	B	G	D	B	G
FINGER	0	2	0	3	1	3	2	3	1	3	0	2	0

G string — D string — A string — E string — A string — D string — G string

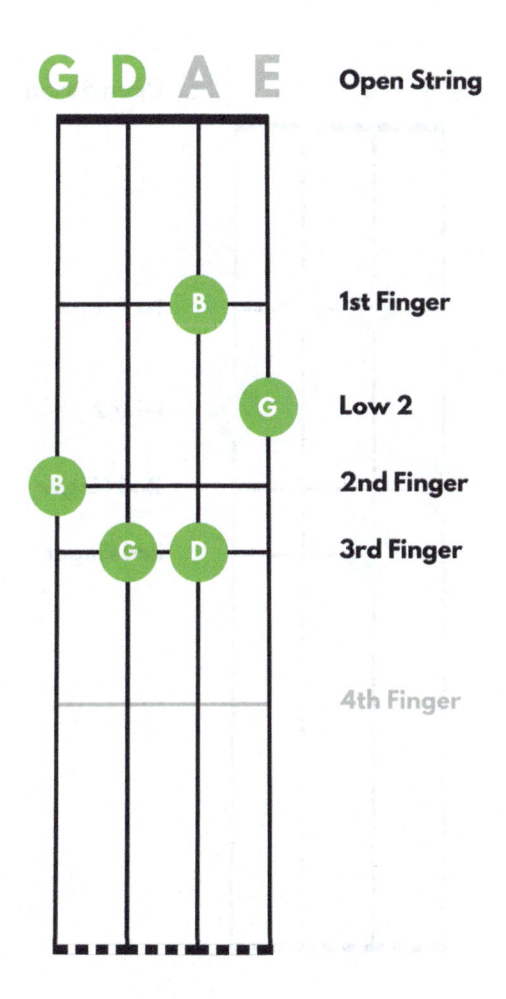

G D A E Open String

- B — 1st Finger
- G — Low 2
- B — 2nd Finger
- G D — 3rd Finger
- 4th Finger

80

G Major Arpeggios
Finger Placement

B

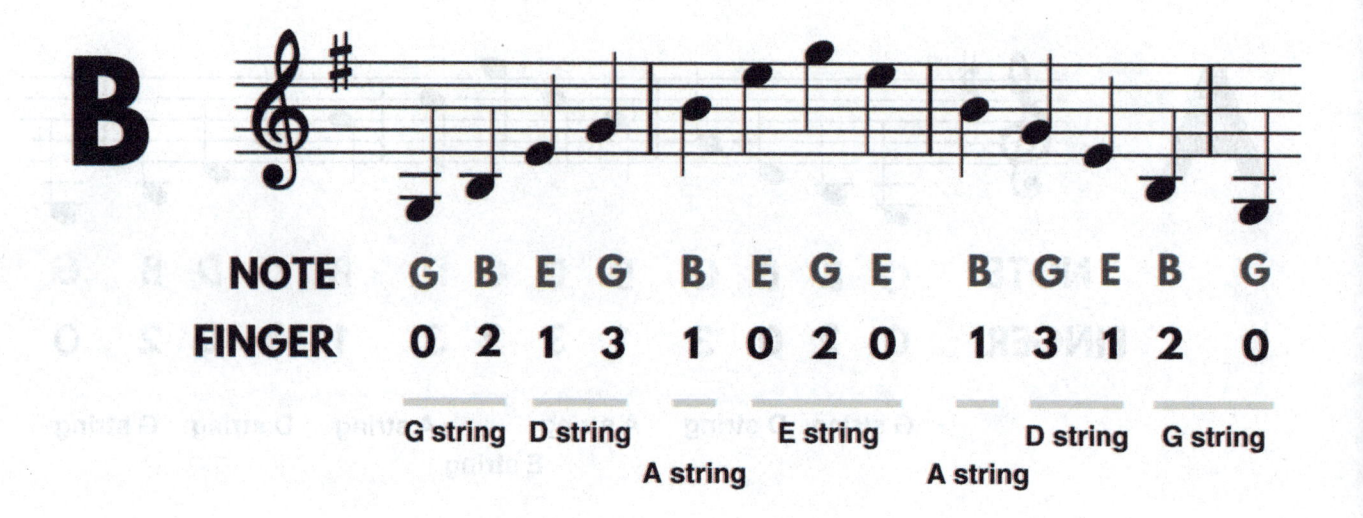

NOTE	G	B	E	G	B	E	G	E	B	G	E	B	G
FINGER	0	2	1	3	1	0	2	0	1	3	1	2	0

G string | D string | A string | E string | A string | D string | G string

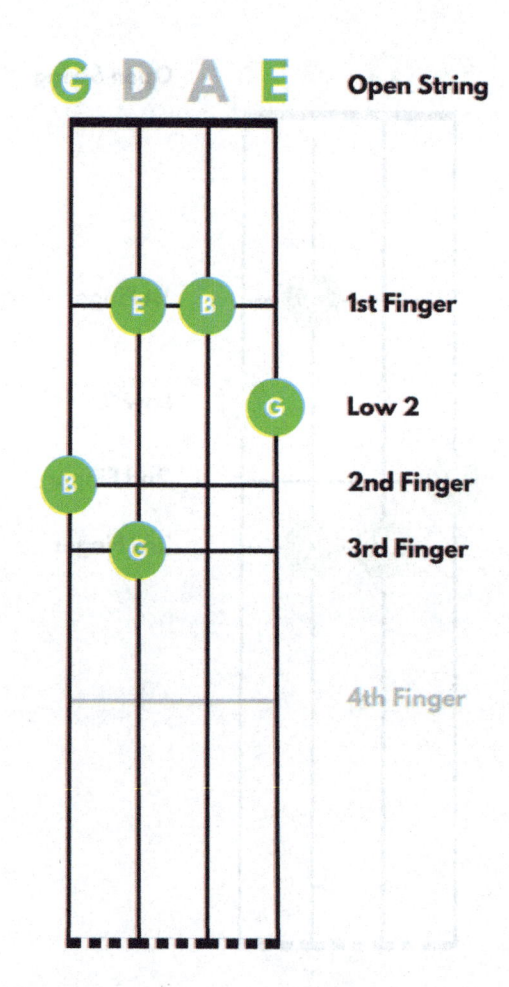

G D A E Open String

- E, B — 1st Finger
- G — Low 2
- B — 2nd Finger
- G — 3rd Finger
- 4th Finger

81

G Major Arpeggios
Finger Placement

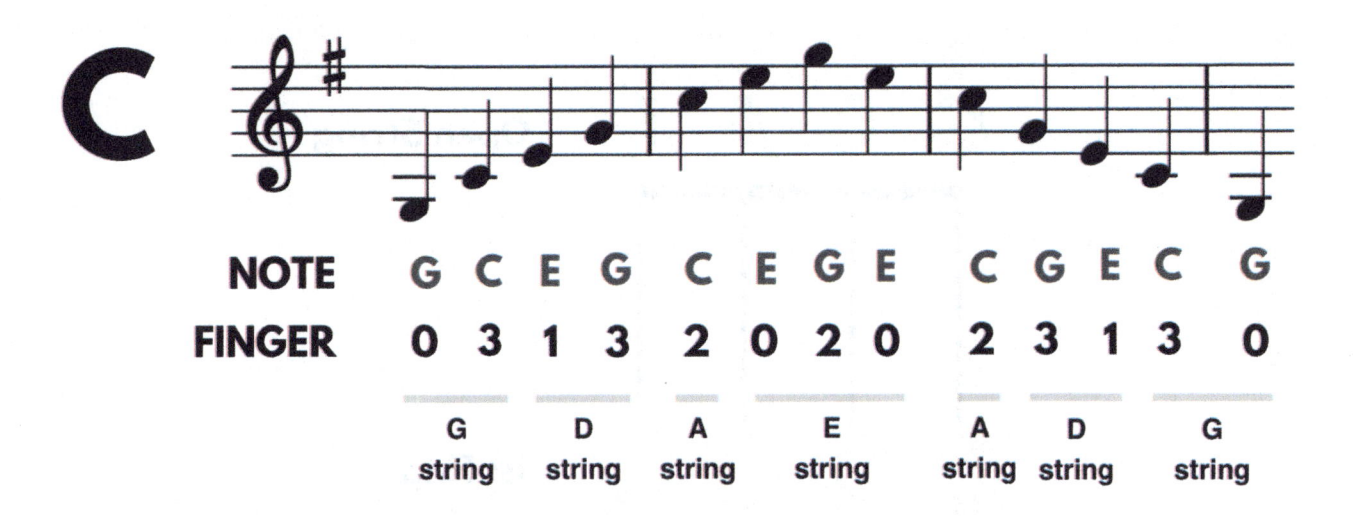

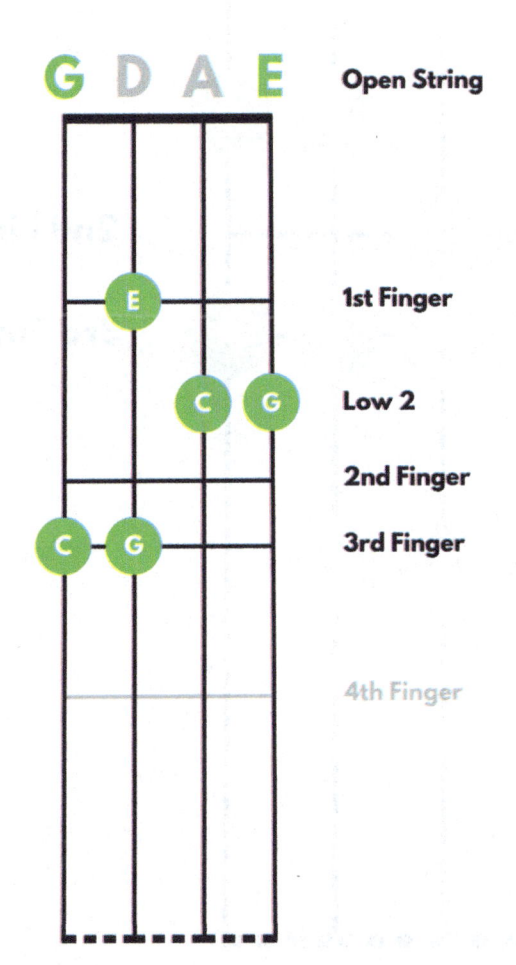

C

NOTE	G	C	E	G	C	E	G	E	C	G	E	C	G
FINGER	0	3	1	3	2	0	2	0	2	3	1	3	0

G string | D string | A string | E string | A string | D string | G string

G D A E Open String

- 1st Finger: E
- Low 2: C, G
- 2nd Finger
- 3rd Finger: C, G
- 4th Finger

82

12. Etude

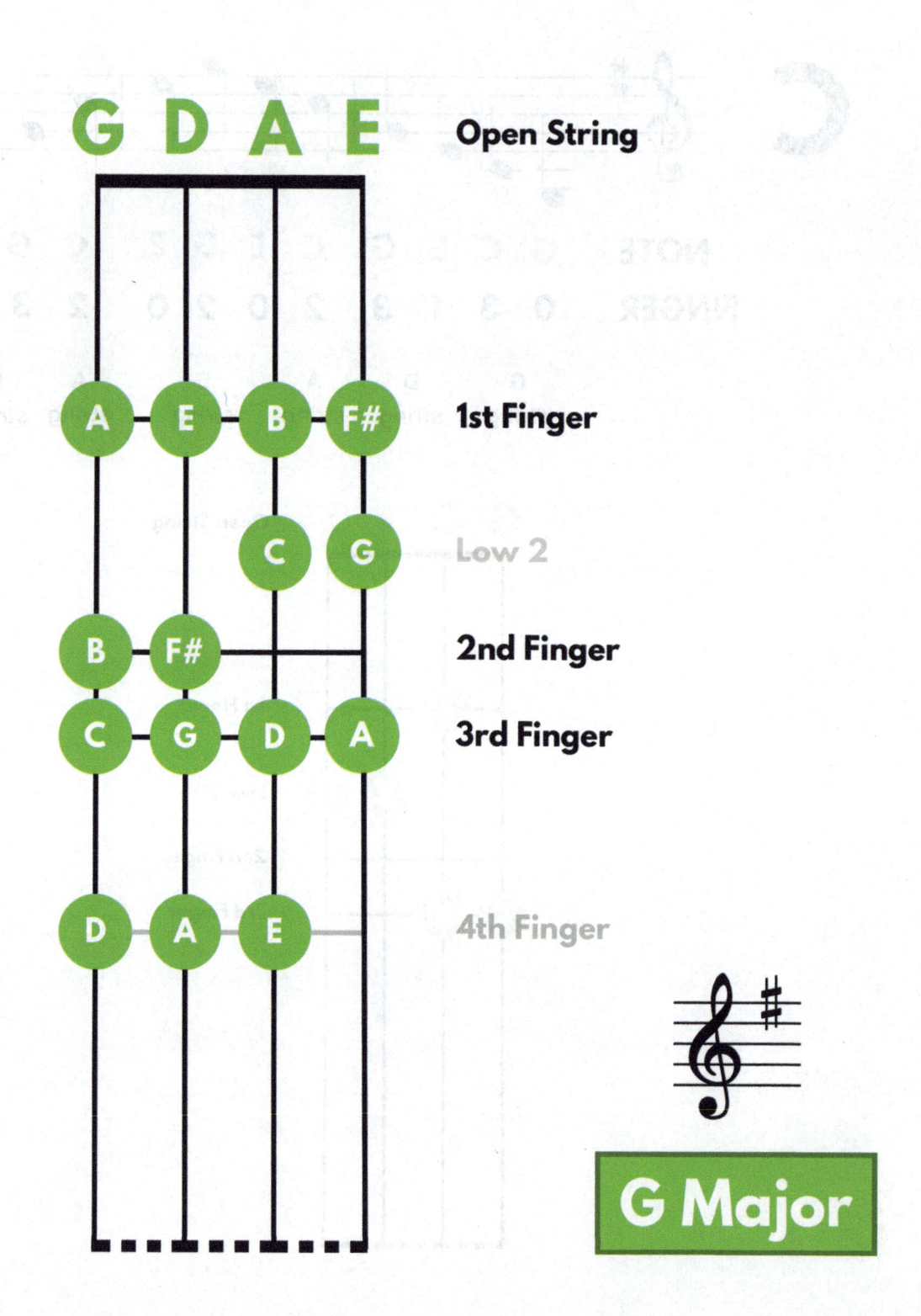

G D A E   Open String

A E B F#   1st Finger

C G   Low 2

B F#   2nd Finger

C G D A   3rd Finger

D A E   4th Finger

G Major

83

13. Minuet No.1

As music gets more complex, sometimes notes are borrowed briefly from another Key to make the music more interesting. These are called accidentals. **Accidentals are noted in black.**

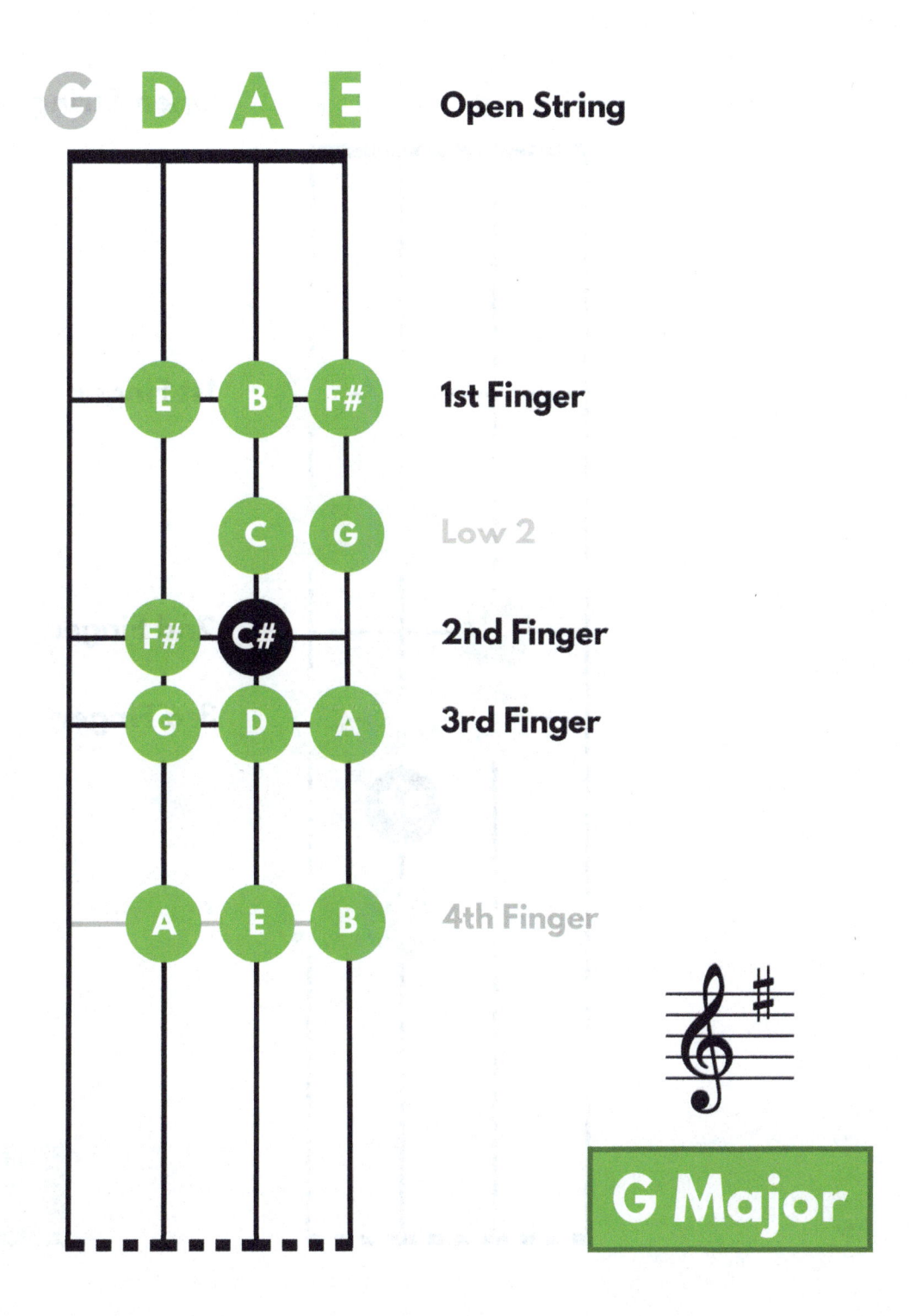

G	D	A	E	**Open String**
	E	B	F#	**1st Finger**
		C	G	Low 2
	F#	C#		**2nd Finger**
	G	D	A	**3rd Finger**
	A	E	B	4th Finger

G Major

14. Minuet No.2

● **Just a reminder! Accidentals are noted in black.**

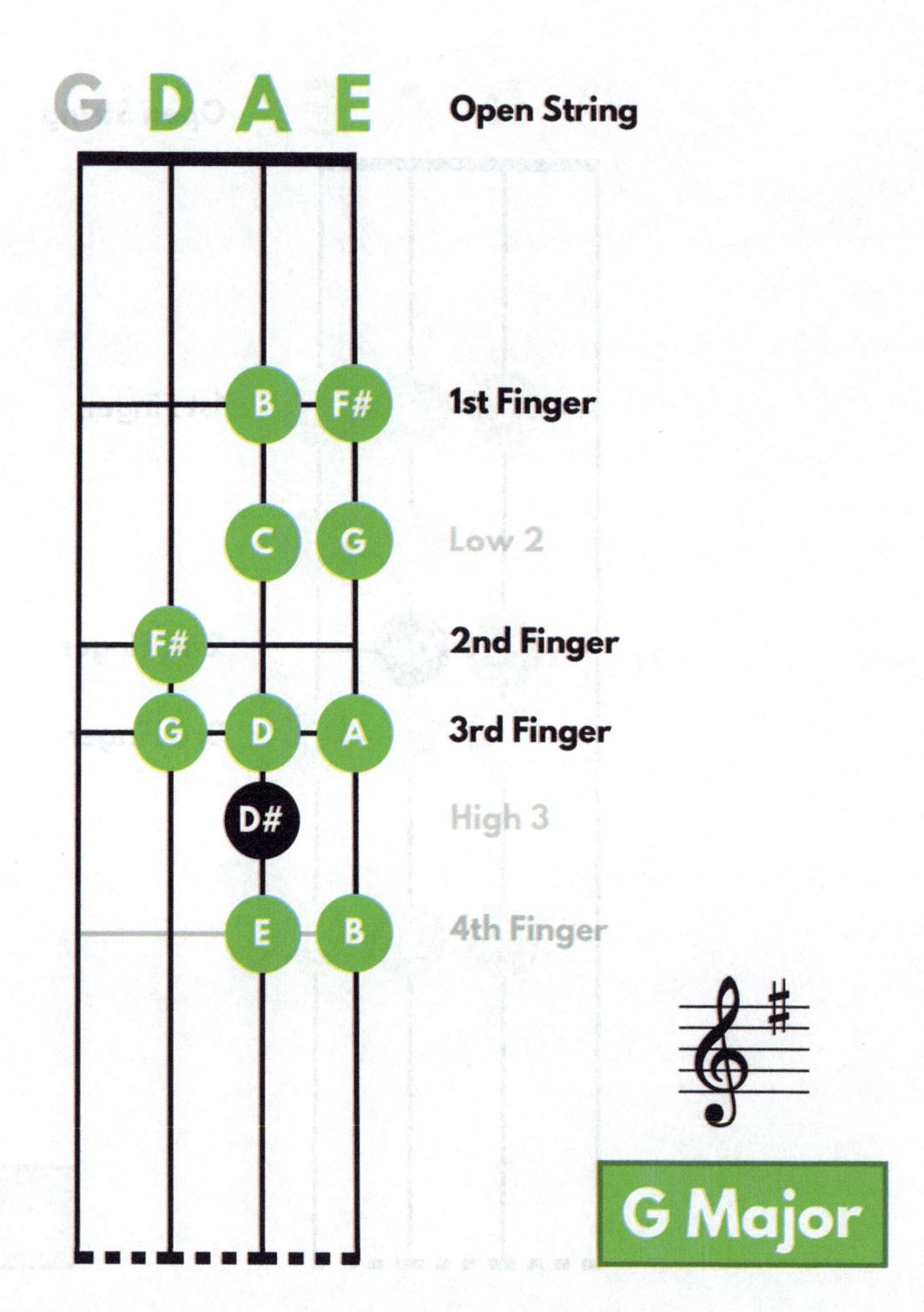

String	G	D	A	E	
					Open String
1st Finger		B	F#		1st Finger
		C	G		Low 2
2nd Finger	F#				2nd Finger
3rd Finger	G	D	A		3rd Finger
		D#			High 3
		E	B		4th Finger

G Major

85

15. Minuet No.3

● Just a reminder! Accidentals are noted in black.

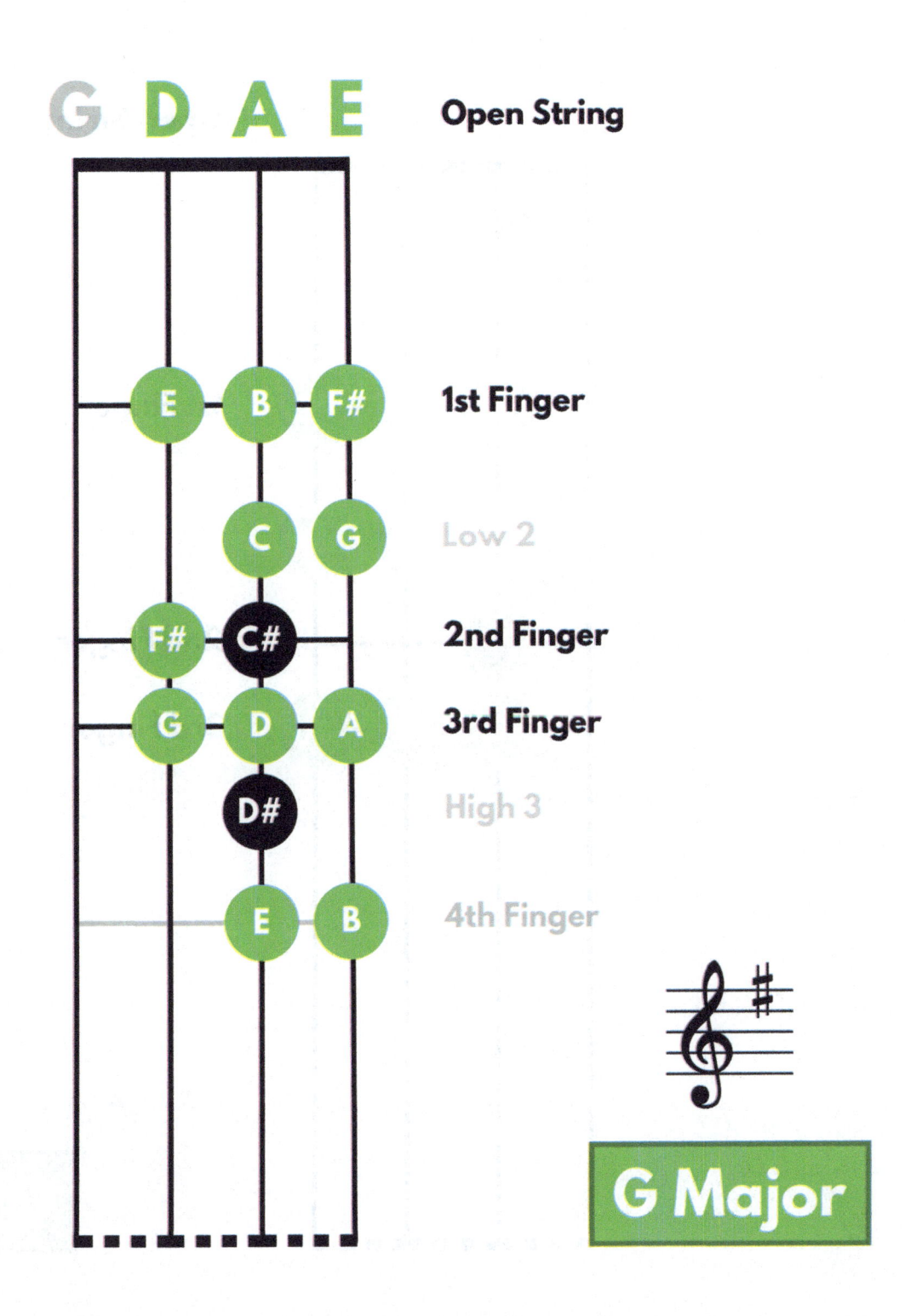

G D A E — Open String

E B F# — 1st Finger

C G — Low 2

F# C# — 2nd Finger

G D A — 3rd Finger

D# — High 3

E B — 4th Finger

G Major

16. The Happy Farmer

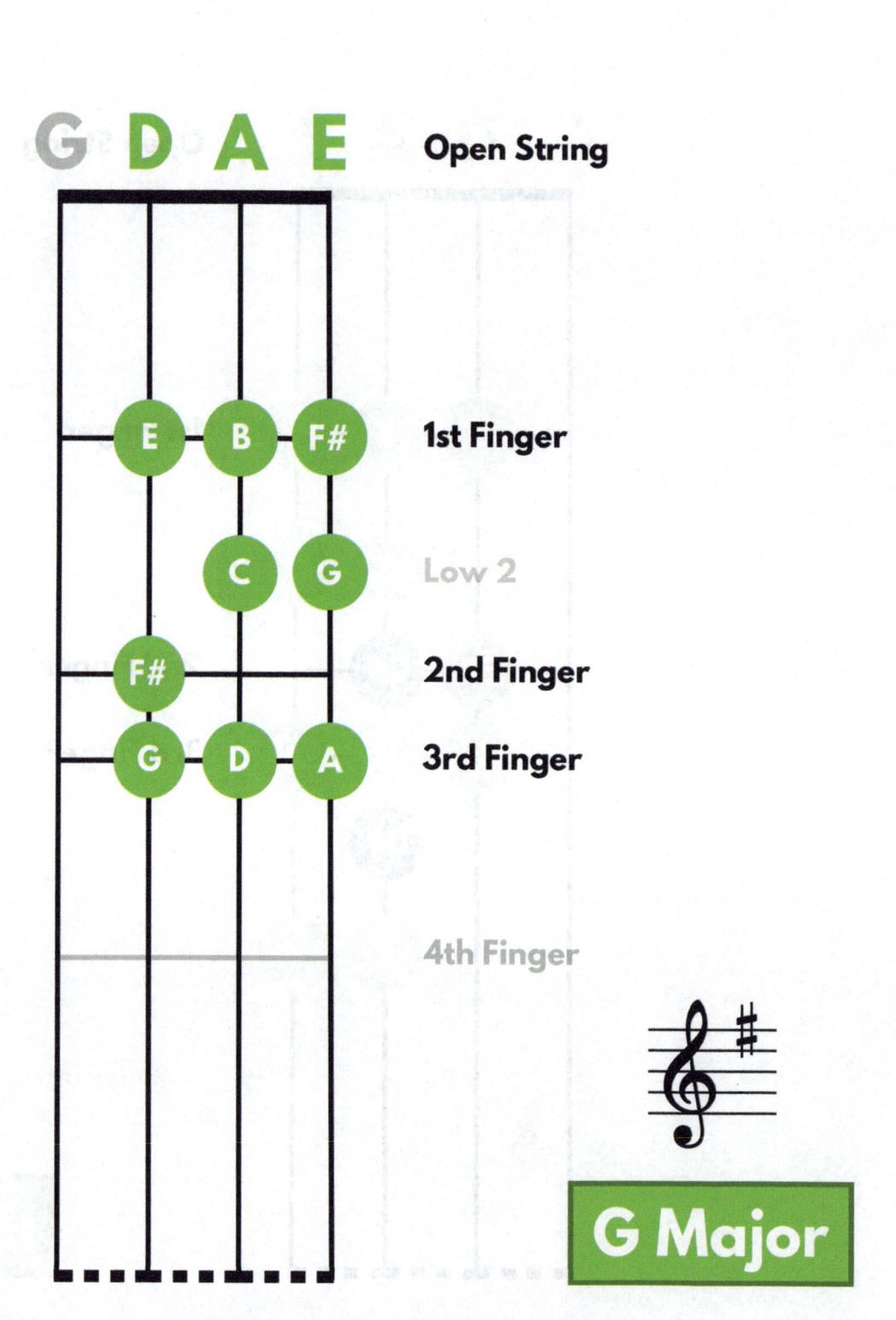

Open String: G D A E
1st Finger: E B F#
Low 2: C G
2nd Finger: F#
3rd Finger: G D A
4th Finger:

G Major

17. Gossec Gavotte

● Just a reminder! Accidentals are noted in black.

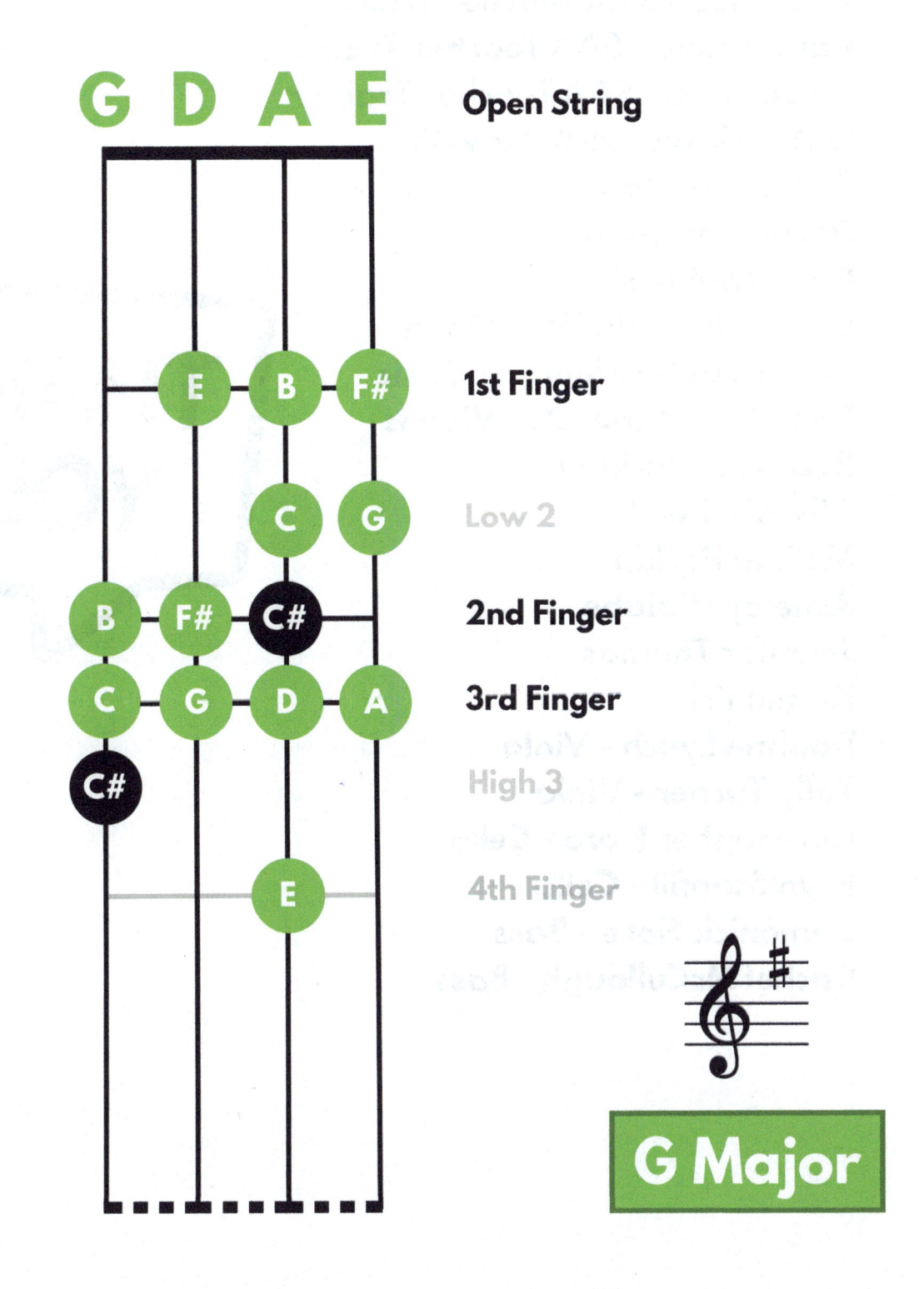

String	G	D	A	E	
Open String	G	D	A	E	
1st Finger		E	B	F#	
Low 2			C	G	
2nd Finger	B	F#	C#		
3rd Finger	C	G	D	A	
High 3	C#				
4th Finger			E		

G Major

Many thanks to all those who helped me get these guides out to help parents and practice partners! My friends and mentors are all to thank for getting this guide into your hands.

Allen Lieb - SAA Teacher Trainer
Pat D'Ercole - SAA Teacher Trainer
Linda Fiore - SAA Teacher Trainer
Gabe Kitayama-Bolkovsky
Russell Fallstad
Doralee Madsen
Pasha Sabouri
Crystal Boyack, Wee Violin
Friends at Day Murray Music
Friends at Adam Day Violins
Rebekah Blackner
Allyson Steed
Melissa Parkin
Asheley Watabe
Jennifer Thomas
Kaitlin Price
Daphne Lynch - Viola
Tally Turner - Viola
Christopher Fiore - Cello
Bryn Stanfill - Cello
Domenick Fiore - Bass
Rachel McCullough - Bass

THANK YOU!

KARI SPICER

STRING COACH

SMART STRING PRACTICE

Kari began Suzuki Violin lessons at age 3 with her grandmother, Doralee Madsen. At age 12, Kari's love of teaching the violin began as she tutored a few of her grandma's violin students for the following six years.

The summer she graduated from high school, Kari started her Suzuki Training at the Intermountain Suzuki String Institute. She is certified in Suzuki Violin Books 1-10 and most of those books she has certified in multiple times!

Kari graduated with a degree in music from Utah State University where she studied under the direction of the renowned Fry String Quartet. She later studied with Simon MacDonald as she pursued Post Graduate work in Violin Performance at the Victoria Conservatory of Music in British Columbia.

In 2011, Kari completed the Suzuki Strings Mentorship Program at the University of Wisconsin at Steven's Point where she studied with Pat D'Ercole. Kari presently studies with Linda Fiore to further her education in teaching the techniques of the violin. In 2022 she completed the "Wee Violin" Workshop with Crystal Boyack and is excited to help parents give their children a fun, new way to practice the Pre-Twinkle steps!

Kari teaches lessons, creates educational materials, and does online coaching for Parents and Practice Partners. Interested in a coach? Send an email to support@smartstringpractice.com or visit **SMARTSTRINGPRACTICE.COM**

Made in United States
Orlando, FL
16 January 2025